ODE ^{TO}_{THE} DODO

by the same author

THE CROCODILE
THE MAGIC CIRCUS
PUSS IN BOOTS
RATSMAGIC
ABECEDARY
THE CHILDREN'S BOOK OF COMIC VERSE *(Batsford)*
THE BUMPER BOOK OF TRUE STORIES *(Private Eye/André Deutsch)*
WAR MUSIC

ODE ^{TO}_{THE} DODO

POEMS FROM 1953 TO 1978

Christopher Logue

JONATHAN CAPE
THIRTY BEDFORD SQUARE LONDON

First published 1981
Copyright © 1981 by Christopher Logue

Jonathan Cape Ltd, 30 Bedford Square, London WC1

This edition contains poems, some revised, from the following
books: *Wand and Quadrant*, 1953; *Devil, Maggot and Son*, 1956;
Songs, 1959; *New Numbers*, 1969; *The Girls*, 1969; *Abecedary*,
1977; the pamphlets: *Singles*, 1973; *Mixed Rushes*, 1974; and
the record *Red Bird*, 1958.

British Library Cataloguing in Publication Data

Logue, Christopher
Ode to the dodo.
I. Title
821'.9'14   PR6023.03801

ISBN 0-224-01892-2
ISBN 0-224-01893-0 Pbk

Printed in Great Britain by The Anchor Press Ltd
and bound by Wm Brendon & Son Ltd
both of Tiptree, Essex

*Go, little book, with all your faults, to one
who, smiling as she puts it down, shall say:
'Sometime his thoughts will permeate my own –
   but not today...'*

Contents

Red Bird *1958*

Songs *1959*

1965

New Numbers *1969*

Wand and Quadrant
1953

Nightpiece

A peacock with a tambourine
sways amid the moonlit green,
whereacross nine ladies go
dancing in a double row.
Figured samite, future gem,
instep glimpsed through cobwebbed hem,
hesitate while slow stars shoot,
fingers arched on peachbowl lute:
led by music ladies come
to the lit pavilion.
There, about the spinal game,
claim creating counterclaim,
see them circle back to back
round the ivory and black.
As the lily reads the jet
see them bless the dark gazette.
And, as music leads the foot,
as the china set the soot,
see them dance by leaf and light
through the solitary night.

Owl's wing soft, and hawk's wing long,
sacred echo, written song,
peacock to oblivion.

More Words than Music

Under the wheel of a momentous star
I begin to write this, my poem, to you,
a mad, imaginary girl; in April, gaining April,
with the sun on the doorstep of Aries.

Thus I unbar my fiction, and prepare
to set in factual order, signs that catch
you where you thrive amid an abstract mass.

And yet how hard it is! You are adroit; you ease,
quickly as speckled algae down a weir,
away from sense until its signs are mere
crosstalk induced by ancient frequencies.

Spin, spin, spin, wheel of my would be mistress,
childlike hopes. Into the air with them!
Into the miles of endless evening sky!
Who falls to nothing through your starry gap
becomes the substance of a later tie.

Dorset Landscape

Green curb that winds abrade;
sea's wallow; thock; outwear;
Barnes and Hardy poets here;
yet in vacant ink arrayed.

The greaseproof moon of Lent.
The tide, ignored by Barnes.
Impermanent. These Purbeck tarns
reflect that lustre Hardy bent

to light his verse, to keep his breath
such love he had — alive and just
in us, for him, such hopeless dust,
until Barnes' kindlier death.

Leader on of evening light,
Lucifer, now Venus starred,
February cliffs but lard
masterpieces based in night.

Now cloud; so low, so pitch,
its icy syrup gags the Head,
10000 years inhabited
ere I learnt which voice was which.

Five Lyrics

I

Winter has flourished and gone
   drinking the last black frost,
the seeds clamber into the sun
   and risen between our toes
have parted the air and the earth.

II

The light is with us. Shall we cross?
   I hear the deepening river flow
beneath us both who go to cast
   our innocence away in love.

III

Small light shall fall
out of these facts,
my skin delights
to be put next
to her who fills
my short sight up
and calls the changes
now and now.

Try, try, and I
have tried again
to act less glad
to less behold

her beck and call
for we may turn
to kissing none
and hindermost
my head shall hang.

IV

I have never been alone,
I have always known that one
body is half humanity
at its minimum.
I can sense, and I can see
all day long men choosing me,
whom I would not choose because
I am given choice by them.
Yet I fit them all. They, me.

My mother told me early on
one choice was mine, one not go wrong;
my body sings a different tune,
to try a dozen out for size.
Still, she frightened me; and then,
as mothers have possessed most men,
have they done the same to them,
but oppositely on?

How much of what is love is fear?
This girl answers from despair;
this girl wants what cost makes chaste;
this, because of ugliness,
goes idle to the grave: alas,
to look the time, to share the day,
by art, by chance, is currency
harder than any nation has.

V

In doubt before her flesh my self
   continually touches her
bright pleats and gussets I beware
   lest timidly I make a girl
what that green skirt adorns my floor.

In this community of two
   how can delight be so complete
yet breed a riddle at its pith?
   how can desire teach lust to bow,
that innocence increases now?

Time says that I shall have no friend
   except his friends that I may like
and friends who isolate his hate.
   How hard to be unlike who was,
and yet like her in purity;
   to weep for whom she could not see,
and hold to those, like me, who err.

Forgive us both, for we must die.

For My Father

A year ago tonight my father died.
   Slow on the year, you bells;
   slow on the year...
And, Master Sun, as you have met your prime
   and sit
   high in the Lion's house,
and have no shadow in your courtyard,
   bequeath
some brief alliteration of your radiance
   to glint this work in words
   that speak of ghosts.

Hector, is Hector dead: and so is he.
His breath, some feathers for an ocean mew;
his hand, his parting wave, some moment where
a rowan's leaf disturbs its morning dew.

"Arrested by mistake — not so released:
   be sure you pray;
no losing throw like hate —
   so keep to love;
who injures you, will not forgive his blow:
   so you must fight;
the wise read letters backwards:
   you must learn;
your hands are not on loan:
   so you must work."
Salute, you lucky mourners, all the dead,
   by your attention to this day,
   for you must think.

Lean priest had not his love
at our last meeting in a London church.

Nor I, nor anyone could lend
a meaning to that requiem
beyond the painful oak.

The host was memory; the wine
examination of the way he grasped
a problem by its rim.
This double sacrament calls in
an Irish Englishman, a dusty road,
his hat tipped halo back, his stick,
Belloc and Chesterton — their verse,
and RLS — his prose;
and never in his life a truthless word.
Indeed, which vexed his boy,
a certain scorn of words; a greater joy
in notes well sung, a stone well thrown,
fine horses managed by a careless rein;
and never in his life a truthless word,
an unjust blow, a mawkish saint;
vengeance, unknown; unknown, complaint.
"It was unjust!" "So I have heard you say.
Think of the justice done you, child. And pray."

Ground, cover him.
Sky, tuck the reflection
of his coffin's lid
into that sparrow's wing.

"Write what you like.
Do something to make other people laugh.
And if at nothing else — at you.
Your temper, boy, will get you thrashed
before you're through.
I cannot bless your Mr Shakespear. True,
he can say it all. And yet
imagine him this afternoon:

The Tragedy of Hitler. Act One, Scene One.
Enter two officers...
Poo poo.''

    Spider
how can I get his most, most gentle voice,
    across the sacrament of death?
    Ant,
from the spire of that grassblade,
can you see larger absences than his?
    Blackbird
behind the maybloom, what is there new
beside the pearly wake of snails,
for me to put upon this paper stone?
"Ah!" he would say, "you should have heard me sing,
before I broke my shoulder whistling."

    Facts fail. The nave grows dim.
    They buried him in rain.
    It cost my mother £50.

    Now we drink sherry
    and recount his worth,
    in this first dusk
    I am alone on earth.

Air

Moon and mandrake
are the fellows
of this heath.

Cairn and gallows
are the signposts
to this park.

Mute and magpie
are the servers
at this feast.

Owl and craken
are the choir
in this dark.

And Tom Beddoes
fills the bagpipe
with cracked breath;

and leads his bride
and bridegroom
to their death.

Devil, Maggot and Son
1956

First Testament

I

Herein some local Heaven,
  our daily bread
is of no joyful harvest taken;
  even by this
  I am discomforted.

Shall I accept my beggary
  and scheme for bread,
when childhood, childhood's perfect city,
  old in my nerves
  makes me discomforted?

Or of an ancient, scatheless age
  report my steeples rang
daily the world to banquet, that
  all evil trashed,
  with all the world, I sang;
or sinfully accept created pain,
  and its relief
as but disgraceful weariness in Cain?
How excellent a base for truthless art!

Our words remain: our signs, our sounds,
  that mixed, make sense.
Nothing particular, of course;
  a pleasure to the memory:
  verse and its common source.

Ten fingers and the vacant tongue
  in futurity to sing
better or worse as I have done:
  merely a childish dread.
Bid memory to prove me wrong!
Here in this all but empty song
  I am discomforted.

II

My class demanded,
and in time was given,
mourning for Finnegan
to peg our graduation.

Beauty indeed it was,
yet truthless beauty seemed,
after the oven door
closed on the worth in war.

All ancient beauty left
only a stinking hint,
Horace to Eliot clipped
to keep their mix intact.

Art: as a special case.
Sense: as a test of art.
Beauty: its proof. Its place
below the famous salt.

Take Rudy Kipling's *If*:
think of its being read
aloud to buoy the hearts
of those that ovens fed.

Beauty as cheap as dirt.
Significance, its scum.
The beatific whores
servicing anyone.

How can we think without?
Such images of grace
from this time forth must cease,
unless, in reading's place,
they can unwillingly
suspend our disbelief.

Sometimes I am Persuaded that Contempt

Sometimes I am persuaded that contempt,
lampoon or pillory, the gallow's stump,
will knock me down the generals in gray suits
cutting their losses with a legal trump.
Before me, contradiction. Accident
enters most easily when rights are quick.
Before I know, the innocent silk is slit
and grievous fingers violate my throat.
I look on him, on her, on them, on it:
my boat is cock-a-block with righteous angry;
some gray with hate, and some with fear, plain gray.
What judge was Noah when he stowed his ark?
Peter I rob; but Paul is left hungry.

Airs and Graces

I

This I ponder
this I weigh
kiss me any
who will say
hand in my hand
come that day.

This I ponder
this I cite
kiss me many
keep the light
heart of my heart
on that night.

II Air for the Witness of a Departure

A high wind blows
over the long white lea
lover
O lover
over the white lea;
knows
who knows where my love is riding?

Thrush in the maybloom
high winds blow
O
over the long white lea;
knows
who knows where my love is riding?
thrush in the maybloom

riding
riding
over the long white lea.

III

Living in you this time
is willingly undone
should you leave this me for this
this or some other one.

So make me safely loveless,
till readily as one
who readily can be
too readily undone,

and I shall love you still
when one beside we three
turns and as simply takes,
takes who takes you from me.

Thus will I love you where
ever it is you lie
in whose uneasy arms
all four shall leave to die.

IV   Lullaby

Child mine. Slumber soon. So drowse.
   My dreamer goes
between these pictures of the moon
through grasses woven with long willow boughs;
   my dreamer goes
where creamy eagles drown
late in the daytime that the light stains rose;
   my dreamer goes
further from voices in the downstairs room
to what he knows, he knows, he knows...

V

My virgin says: Spring wind,
no one has introduced us.
Why do you part my curtains?

My bride says: Summer wind,
carry who married a fatherly lover
far from who promised a liverish son.

My mother says: Warm autumn wind,
you visit me so rarely;
why lift my dress tonight?

My patient says: I am alone.
Should you come near me, winter wind,
divorce my heart and bone.

Six Sonnets

I

The cherubim tune up their instruments.
Our dance begins with sight, proceeds to sense,
and soon our words convert such facts to law,
and we are loved; who were not loved before.
The cherubim tune up their instruments.
She moves my flesh; my flesh moves hers to speak;
thus in her voice my boastful voice can score:
Our love is that eternity men seek.
The cherubim tune up their instruments.
Starting these verses on a winter's day,
enliteralised our end by summer's peak;
mindful what we became could not dismay
the hope that neither time nor place invents.
The cherubim tune up their instruments.

II

Seek her. Undo her mouth. Eat her red mouth.
Be gluttonous. Be avid. Gorge her mouth.
And in these swinish instants claim your mouth
rivals creation, occupies the air —
as much her meaty breath, as of that South
(her insegmental voice, her hemisphere)
before known only by its songs and fruit.
In what condition do you find yourself?
Hairs growing on your heart? Ambition, mute?
Breath, brain, bone, background, beauty, beast, and brute,
all swarming to inform her fragrant tilth?
Then integrate these particles, and swear:
Zero plus one — no logic less that pair.
Godlike that such alternatives are rare.

III

Our desire moves in a lewd orbit.
Together we might float a planet.

Notice her eyes; they take the light like dew.
Notice the way she turns her head; O few
immortal scribblers glimpsing fictions still,
only if Aphrodite brightened thee
(patient as locks on ruins on God's Hill)
with such a glance, you would not envy me
for once; who, if she looks aside, acts ill.

And in the abstract of her walk, tip toe,
(some do in love — this girl in love walks so)
notice, who still retain an earthly view,
all the momentous secrecy of two
in whom lust finds subjection, and runs true.

IV

William, song's king, was wrong: love is time's fool,
and starred in separation. Left alone
grinds out his blame between the local stone
and the horizon's rim — for she was fair;
a fraud to patient others, well aware
who now cries wrong, was wrong; not only fool,
but Tom against the World; one soft on fear;
his lobby, dark; self-pity's Senator;
who would not bid; who could not bide; who sped
her on her way; away; but longs to hear:
Think of her faults. Consider her as dead.
Who was so straight; so fair; she almost said:
Love ground your crumb, Fe Fi, to please his head.
Now eat the crust, Fo Fum, of what you bred.

V

Meat me to slay, out of abominable
pity for abstract I? Salacious crime
exemplified by mediocrity.
All reasons for self-sake lie in your will
to her? Poo. Poo. Why pick on her? Take Bill
the Big, the Master, what you will, and see
lies pitched through light by paratactic sign,
that self-same kind of vengeful sanity,
successfully unjust, to the n'th degree,
spite reaping time, reduced by time to thee.
O graphospasmic penpusher, beware!
Love's angel, naming interested fools,
may, as he passes, say of your despair:
The devil's martyr drowns in shallow pools.

VI

For God's sweet sake forgive that parting black
I gave. Part of that part? One loving jot?
Child, I am no Elizabethan hack
spicing his dalliance in a sonnet's pot;
but instantaneous ape on hairpin knees,
with leash in hand, and scientific wrong:
Miss Right, be good enough to take these keys,
my words, my iconciliation...

It will not do; for she will join the dead
unwillingly as me, but with her hope,
as in her final word, on yet ahead:
Death's finger points me on. I shall not dote.
For anything I owe, take what we shed.
Why should we care what was if you are read?

Red Bird
1958
After Pablo Neruda

I

Lithe girl; brown girl;
the sun that woos apples
and stiffens the wheat
made your body with joy.

Your tongue, like a red bird
dancing on ivory; your lips
with the smile of water.

Tantalise the sun
if you dare, it will leave
shadows that match you
everywhere.

Lithe girl; brown girl;
nothing draws me towards you.
And the heat within you
beats me home
like the sun at high noon.

Knowing these things; perhaps
through knowing these things,
I seek you out.

Daft for the sound of your voice,
or the brush of your arms
against wheat, or your step
among poppies grown under water.

II

Steep gloom among pine trees.
The waves surge, breaking. Slow lights
that interweave. A single bell.
And as the day's end falls into your eyes,

the earth starts singing in your body
as the waves sing in a white shell.

And the rivers sing within you;
and light flows outwards on them;
as you direct them;
whither you make them run;
and I must follow after like a hare
running reared upright to the hunter's drum.

You turn about me like a belt of cloud.
Your silence, although stupid,
mocks the hours I lay
troubled by nothing. Your arms
translucent stones wherein I lie
exhausted. And future kisses die.

Last: your mysterious voice folds close
echoes that shift throughout the night.
Much as the wind that moves,
darkly, over the profitable fields,
folds down the wheat
for all its height.

III

That you may hear me, my words
    narrow occasionally,
like gull tracks in the sand;
    or I let them become
tuneful beads mixed with the sound
    of a drunk hawk's bell.
And soft as grapeskin, yes,
    softer than grapeskin I make them;
which is a kind of treachery
    against the painful world.

Before you came to me,
    words were all you now occupy;
and knowing you now they know more

than ever they learnt from that sadness.
Yet, sometimes
   the force of dead anguish
still drags them; and, yes,
   malevolent dreams still, at times,
overwhelm them; and then
   in my bruised voice you hear
other bruised voices; old agues crying
   out of old mouths.

So do not be angry at this,
   lest the wave of that anguish
drowns me again while I sit
   threading a collar of beads for your wrist,
softer than grapeskin,
   hung with a drunk hawk's bell.

IV

Drunk as drunk on turpentine
from your open kisses,
your wet body wedged
between my wet body
and the strake of our boat
that is made out of flowers —
feasted, we guide it
(our fingers like tallows adorned with gold metal)
over the sky's hot rim;
the day's last breath in our sail.

Pinned by the sun between solstice
and equinox; drowsy, entangled together,
we drifted for months and woke
with the bitter taste of land on our lips
(eyelids all sticky) and longed for lime
and the sound of a rope
lowering its bucket down a well. Then,
came we by night to the Fortunate Isles
and lay like fish
under the net of our kisses.

V

Sometimes you seem like dead,
when you say nothing.

Or is it? – *heard the things you say*
but just could not be bothered to reply.

And your eyes, sometimes,
move outside of you,
watching the two of us,

yes,

as if (after you turn towards the wall)
somebody's kisses stopped your mouth.

VI

My fingers have crept
down your body's white map
like patient spiders;

and my tongue has forked
self-pitying tales
to make you mad.

Where once I brought
wooed fruit and well cut stones
to please us both,

and well worn thoughts
in well placed words that won
more praise than they were worth

but made you glad,
now all I fetch
impatiently you shun,

are never glad.

Nor will you go away.
And nor will I.

How heavily this lovely summer's day
sits on our graceless hands.
Most shameful we.

Your stupid loveliness;
my stupid wit.
A pair enough to try

the patience of a saint,
or make a passing angel spit.
Ah we, ah we.

VII

Tonight, I write sadly. Write,
for example: Little grasshopper,
shelter from the midnight frost
in the scarecrow's sleeve;
advising myself.

Tonight, I write so wearily. Write,
for example: I wanted her,
and at times it was me she wanted. Write:
The rain we watched last fall —
has it fallen this year, too?

She wanted me, and at times it was her
I wanted. Yet it is gone, that want.
What's more, I do not care.
It is more terrible than my despair
at losing her.

The night, always vast,
grows enormous without her.
And my comforter's tongue

talking about her,
is a red fox barred by ivory; well,
does it matter I loved too weak to keep her?
The night ignores such trivial disputes.
She is not here. That's all.

Far off, someone is singing.
And if to bring her back I look,
and I run to the end of the road,
and I shout, shout her name,
my voice comes back; the same, but weaker.

This night is the same night; it whitens
the same tree; it casts the same shadow.
It is as dark, as long, as deep, and as endurable
as any other night.

It is true: I don't want her.
But perhaps I want her...
Love's not so brief that I forget her,
thus. Nevertheless, I shall forget her, and,
alas, as if by accident,
a day will pass in which
I shall not think about her even once.
And this, the last line I shall write her.

Songs
1959

The Song of the Dead Soldier

In school I learnt of thirty kings,
   their ways, their wars – if these were won;
and out, among some other things,
   about an island in the sun
   where the Queen of Love was born.

At seventeen the postman brought
   into the room – my place of birth –
some correspondence from the Crown
   demanding that with guns I earn
   the modern shilling I was worth.

Lucky for me that I could read.
   Lucky for me the Captain said:
You'll see the world for free, my son.
   You're posted to an island, John,
   where the Queen of Love was born.

So twenty weeks went by and by
   my back was straightened up, my eye
as true as any button shone;
   and nine white-bellied dolphins led
   our ship of shillings through the sun.

Landing beneath our guns, and clad
   in camouflage – at £60
the best bespoken off-the-peg –
   our bootsteps crossed her cowrie bounds,
   and she, Love's Queen, our loveless flag,

our cause, our curfew – fifed with jeers,
   our blancoed cage, where, when we sat
as if we were the prisoners,

I drank my eyes clean out my head
and wet my shilling's cheek with fears.

Next day, sky high, stud bright, the sun
between our thicket bayonets clicked;
and china white our faces shone
that kept her precincts — mine among —
black cherry regulation strict.

No hint my china head would catch
the needle of that sniper's V;
or his deaf eye my I might scratch;
or empty brilliance smother me
as sunlight does a lighted match:

but thus they did. And as I fled
from light to light through nothingness,
Love's fictive Regent cruised the abyss
and caught me in her arms, and said:
Shilling misspent, I ask but this
to keep you from beneath above.
Dismiss the memory of your flesh,
your name, your nationality,
and be my sovereign soldier, love,
now and for all eternity.

And thus I did.

The Ass's Song

In a nearby town
there lived an Ass,

who in this life
(as all good asses do)

helped his master,
loved his master,

served his master,
faithfully and true.

Now the good Ass worked
the whole day through,

from dawn to dusk
(and on his Sundays, too)

so the master knew
as he rode to mass

God let him sit
on the perfect Ass.

When the good Ass died
and fled above

for his reward
(that all good asses have)

his master made
from his loyal hide

a whip with which
his successor was lashed.

The Song of the Outsider

This city and its citizens are green.
Quickly, those who come from far off
and enter this city, turn green.
Many have rushed here, suffering dangers unnumbered,
just to be green. And others, with contacts,
with money, with skills that are wanted,
have brought their children, dogs, and servants,
so that all they possess shall be green.
Only one dweller herein,
only one, has not become green.
How much he would give to be green!
If he could be green, why—nothing would matter.
He suffers from this. He may well go *Pop!*
At night, beneath the huge green stars,
he goes about crushing young greenies
to ease his hatred and his fears.
It is bad to do this. He knows it is bad.
And thinking of his evil deeds he sheds
deeply felt tears. If only I were green, he says,
life would be like a children's game.

The Story of Two Gentlemen and the Gardener or
How to Prove the Sun

One spring, the old Philosopher, feeling his bones
to be almost dry, wished to retire. For 60 years
his search for the truth had been constant;
but standing at the door is hard. And because
the leaders of his country were speaking again
about loyalty and sacrifice, the old Philosopher knew
misery was on the way; and to spend a year or two
at rest, in the palace gardens, he must hurry.

He cleaned his shoes. Then, carrying his necessaries
(that is to say, almost nothing) he walked
for one last time among men and streets
he had never understood, towards the huge iron gates,
and showed his references. They asked him to wait.
Later, as he had given no trouble to the authorities,
had been pleased by small mercies, patient,
confining his efforts to logic, and similar things
not of great interest to his neighbours, he was admitted.

The ladies-in-waiting washed the old Philosopher
and gave him a change of clean linen. One said:
Why have you come to the palace gardens?
What will you do among statues and lawns?
These were questions he had anticipated. First,
I shall talk to my nephew, the Poet, he answered.
Luckier than me, he is still young, and has lived
herein since passing his examination. Second,
I shall die. As for why I am here — is it not true
that the pawns are nearest the Queen?

And he passed out of sight round a mulberry tree.

That night, while leafing through each other's books,
these gentlemen agreed to meet each day
and state their thoughts in talk and talk about.

If Monday was for *Metre—Fact Or Not?*
then Tuesday's would be *Validating What?*
The old Philosopher was glad to get such terms.
He unpacked his bundle and went to sleep.

Fresh on the palace steps they met next day,
above them the white sun, and arm in arm they glided down
over the thousand-year-old lawn
between stone lords and naked dames until
they reached a shady place and set their backs
against the garden wall.

Consider, the Philosopher began, the sun.
How can we know if it is truly sun? —
and, if it truly is, is truly there?

And if, good Sir, the sun is there today,
the poet said to keep things moving on,
is it the sun that we saw yesterday?
O, nephew, if tomorrow it comes up,
no certainty exists it is the sun
that warms us now. Alas, for us
the nourishment of doubt is endless.

And certain of their doubt they thought of 40 winks.

Permit me, Sirs, a voice beside them said,
to clear this matter up.
And opening their eyes they saw a gardener.

And then, as they were courteous men,
they let the gardener speak, but cautioned him
that thoughts identical, but more complex, than these
had lasted wisdom's kin for centuries.

So the gardener told them how the sun
is round is gold is vast is hot is beautiful,
useful and constant, old, adored and far,

and how they would, seeing the age was hard,
circumnavigate it 70 times — or less,
and how the sun is rich, perpetual, generous...

At length the old Philosopher held up his hand:
If we agreed with all you say, my friend,
nothing, alas, is changed; our doubt, our doubt;
your proof, no proof. And what is more,
the sun is going down. Your point stays moot.

One moment, Sirs. My proof, the gardener said,
is incomplete. Would you return, tomorrow, say,
and let me finish? Yes?

Next day, this time at dawn, the pair of them,
a little cold inside, waited until the gardener showed.
Now, said the old Philosopher, conclude.
So the gardener told them how the sun is round,
is vast is hot, useful and constant, old, adored, and —
Stop! the Poet said. All this we heard before.

Indeed, the gardener said, before I can conclude,
you first must prove yourselves to be
the gentlemen that I met yesterday.
How else can I be absolutely sure
you are who heard the opening of my proof?

To My Fellow Artists

I

Today, it came to me. How you, my friends
who write, who draw and carve,
friends who make pictures, act, direct,
finger delicate instruments,
compose, or fake, or criticise — how,
in the oncoming megaton bombardments,
all you stand for will be gone
like an arrow into hell.

II

It is strange, and yet
if I tell you how the sunlight glitters
off intricate visions etched into breastplates
by Trojan smiths, you say: Yes! Yes!
And if I say:
around my bedposts birds have built their nests
that sing: No! No! —
or say: when I flog salt, it rains;
when I sell flour, it blows —
you feel my hopelessness; and more,
you understand my words.

But if I speak straight out, and say:
infatuates to local immortality,
distinguished each from each by baby pains
you measure against baby pain, you stand
to lose the earth and look alike
as if you spat each other out, you say:
Logue grinds his axe again. He's red —
or cashing in... And you are right:

I have an axe to grind. Compared to you,
I'm red — and short of cash. So what?
I think, am weak, need help, must live,
and will — with your permission — live.
Why should I seek to puzzle you with words
when your beds are near sopping with blood?
And yet I puzzle you with words.

III

If (as many as you do) you base
all of your hope, all of that hope
necessary to make a work of art
on unborn generations, start
hunting for a place to hide the art
you will create in privation.

Consider, my fellows,
how all the posh goodies inside our museums,
stones, books, things we have stolen,
think of them turned to instant dust
one dusk between six and six-ten.

It is true: they will say you are fools
who know nothing of politics.
Women and artists must keep out of politics.
They will suggest (politely... politely...)
that the length of your hair pre-empts your sanity.
They will, with their reason,
prove your unreasonableness;
though you are drugged by rationality.

They will do all in their power
(and their power is great)
to shut you up, until
recommending your wife's sensual niceties,
or lamenting her, loose in the hilts,
you thrive like milestones for whom
the Queen's green £s were contagious.

IV

Listen, I beg you. Six days ago
a paper called *The Sunday Times*
revealed, with witless candour,
their dead thoughts:

You are confused about destruction, yes?
they said. And then — recommending the death of the country
in the name of the country: *We shall bomb,*
if bomb we must, bomb like King Billy,
for the British have something to die for.
No mention was made of something to live for.
Saying (in the names of loyalty, faith, integrity):
How vile they are who wish to live here
minus the local notion of democracy.
Not speaking of those who wish to die here.

The death before dishonour, boys;
the death before gestapo, boys;
the death before a tyrant, boys;
the death before *The Sunday Times*.

But where is the dishonour, gestapo, or tyrant?
And who wants to dishonour or govern a cinder?
My friends,
how difficult it is for those who speak
out of anger to answer those who speak
out of complacency.

And yet, imagine a horror
and perpetrate horrors because of it,
is called mad.

Think desolation
and create desolation because of it,
is called mad.

Thus the Ripper and Christie
thought of whores.
Thus they think of our country.

V

So do you agree with them
Spender, and Barker, and Auden?
And you, my newly married master, Eliot —
will you adopt their lie by silence,
and having sold our flesh to war
bequeath our bones to God?
Or are there two sides to *this* question?

But I fear we are easily beaten.
So where shall we hide them, our treasures?
Uncertain the disused chalk pit;
uncertain the bank's steel vault;
and the holds of ships are uncertain.

We must beg for permission
to hang our paintings underground,
to store our books and stones in mines;
but the rents will be high underground,
and I doubt if we can afford them.

Perhaps they will let a few of us hide
in the negative silos, 1000 feet down,
where, beside telephones, uniformed men
await fatal words.
We must not be afraid to ask;
for works concerning the private heart
will not alter devoted experts.

But let us remember to leave behind
permanent signs. Signs that are easily read.
Signs that say: So deep,
beneath so many feet of stone,
is a poem expressing refinement of taste,
a book about logic, a tape of quartets,
and a picture of the painter's wife.

Then can our six-handed grandsons,
our unborn consolation,
discover that we too, had art.

And those who dare look
over the crater's jagged rim,
may, in the evening, climb down
into the mauve bowl of London,
and dig.
While their guards watch out
for tyrants, and food, and sun.

Think, men of no future,
but with a name to come.

Professor Tuholsky's Facts

Once upon a little planet,
a neat, provincial planet, set
deep in the galactic sticks,
there lived an interesting thing
called *Man*.

Man had two legs, and two *Convictions*:
one was called *Luck*,
which he described as *Good* when things went *Right*.
The other one he used when things went *Wrong*.
This was called *Religion*.

Man was vertebrate, bipodic, often bald,
and had a *Soul* that never died.
Also — to check his overconfidence —
he had his *Leaders*, and his *Fellow Countrymen*.

Man ate a lot:
plants, fish, animals, birds, snails...
in fact, he ate whatever he could kill.
Occasionally he ate his *Fellow Men* —
but this was rare.

Each man had a liver, a heart, a brain,
and a *Flag*.
These were his vital organs.
On these his life depended.

I have no doubt that there were men alive
with only half a liver;
some had no heart;
and many had no brain.

But a man without a flag?
Impossible!

Man was the most *Useful* of earthly creatures.
Cheerfully he raised the value of shares,
cheerfully he died a soldier's death,
or committed spectacular crimes —
and thereby sold innumerable newspapers
(all of which have now vanished).

Many admired *Human Character* —
but it was split.
One half was known as *Male*,
and did not want to think;
the other half was known as *Female*,
in whom thinking was discouraged.

Yet both had this in common:
they were full of fear.
They were afraid of death, of debt,
of loneliness, of failure, and of war.
But most of all they feared their *Fellow Man*.

Of course, some men were different:
Thinkers, or *Revolutionaries*, or *Saints*.
However, these were few; and they
were quickly crucified, or shot, or poisoned.

Next week we study Dogs.

Various Rules

I Understand Others

Do not be frightened:
if you meet a poet on the road,
  give him your poem;
if you meet a painter on the road,
  give him your painting;
if you meet a merchant on the road,
  give him your money.

II Good Taste

Travelling, a man met a tiger, so...
he ran. And the tiger ran after him
thinking: How fast I am...

But the road thought: How long I am...
Then they came to a cliff, and the man
grabbed at an ash-root and swung down

over its edge. Above his knuckles, the tiger;
at the foot of the cliff, its mate. Two mice,
one black, one white, began to gnaw the root.

And by the traveller's head grew one
juicy strawberry. So... hugging the root
the man reached out and plucked the fruit:

  how sweet it tasted!

III Be Practical

Before bombardment
there lived by me

a maker of exquisite dolls who gained
living enough from his sales.

And he told his wife:
Hereafter our dolls
will be made with their hands tucked away.
This will save clay.

The enterprise worked.
So he said: Wife,
in future our dolls will be made sitting down.
This will save time.

And his plan worked well.
So he said: Let us make
dolls with their heads bent over in sleep.
This will save cash.

And when they were done
the dollmaker's wife,
examining one before they were sold, said:
Now let us hire some men to make dolls
while we tour the world.

IV Educate

Say to the child: This is one...
showing him an apple: This is two...
showing him a word: This is three...
and you turn and you walk away
   with his mother and his ball.

V Understand Yourself

Each day, deep in his University,
a scholar shouted: Master!
and answered himself: Yes, Sir?
Then shouted out: Work harder!

and answered: Yes, Sir...
And after: Do not be fooled by others!
Answering: Yes, Sir. Yes, Sir.

VI Observe Details

When you visit the Humans
who stick to their fruitless cinder,
    be sure to see,
down by the nice little bar where they sell
    roast mutton and girls,
the armless Army man who sings
    How Tranquil The Evening
as he points his leg at the moon.

VII Obedience

A writer lived alone among
those who found words to be their enemies:
still, they praised his modest life.

A brimming girl lived in his street
who suddenly was four months gone.
Nor would she name the man until
her father whipped her arse; whereon
she gave the writer's name.
Then family, and street, and all
came angrily to him.

"Is that so?" and "Is that so" was all he said.
Thus when the child was born they gave it him,
who had by now lost all his reputation there,
which only somewhat troubled him —
since those who live by others die from farting.

However; with the child he took great care,
learning its needs, sharing his time with it,
and teaching it ("What else?") to be a human.

Within a natural year who bore it said
a handsome carpenter had laid her first
and now that he and she were wed
could they have the child back?

Shamefaced her father knocked to know,
with the neighbours behind him.
And the writer, giving the child again, said: "Is that so?"

Lullaby

Here is the trapdoor,
here is the rope,
here is the convict,
here is the judge and
here the skilled hangman;
here is a juror,
    and eleven more
    sensible humans
    not courted before.

Here is the judgment,
here is the crime,
    go from the prison
    into the lime.
Here are three Sundays,
here is the Warden,
here is the chaplain,
    and coming behind him,
    the convict's weight
    and how he will die;
    dutiful lights
    in the hangman's eye.

Here is the throat;
here is the knot
    as long as your forearm;
here is the spring from
here to eternity
    dressed in a hood.
    And be it a man
    or a woman they shit
    and they come

as they swing
and the soul goes adrift.

Here is the hangman,
here is his garden,
here he is sleeping,
this is his number.
    And one of the jurors
    has given a daughter
    to comfort his slumber.

The Story of the Road

Imagine yourself in a country, poor —
not as ours is — but poor for better than bread.
Some men have not worked for ten years, and some
(the youngest) never.
There are many priests hereabout. Some, good men;
some pleased to bless the Lord Mayor's goat, in a land
shaped like a triangle, set in known water,
host to a host but owned by less than 1000 men
from its limestone base to the cone at its top,
to the water's edge and beyond.

Well, one day, off the weekly boat
that brings mail, tobacco, and news,
a man called Daniel came to see
where his father had worked on the railway.
A girl was having her third by the pump,
and it died by the pump while Daniel looked,
shook his big head, walked by, and later that day
rented a house in the stinking quarter,
and wrote to his girl: Either come, or it's off.

It is March. Early spring. Some buy cheap meat;
when it boils you scent their extravagance.
And all day long this Daniel poses questions:
such as when, for how long, for how much, and for whom
(aside from themselves) they fish. And they said:
We do not flinch at the shadow of a whip,
or the whip... So the child died? So what? We are brave.
And Daniel (who is cautious) saw their courage
and was glad; but also saw their trembling hands.
A message came that night. It said: It's off.

Long night. No moon. Still blackness round
the low white houses with wide throats.

Wise people sleep. But some (not always young)
with energy enough to scorn their pain,
sit listening while the fish thieves trawl the coast,
and the newly spawned are caught with the two-years-old,
and the autumn shoal is lifted in the spring.

Six weeks of questioning and soon
wherever Daniel goes many children go
and not a few police. One sometime fisherman said:
Statistic? What's a statistic? Well... from this town
350 sometime fishermen got
3000 years of gaol between them but
between them only 50 years of school.
Even the chief policeman laughed, till Daniel said:
Tomorrow we strike—yes? Yes. They wrote that down.

Some people had said: He will stay for a week.
He will stay for a month. He will starve—
for poverty's catching.
But the almonds had turned when he said:
Tomorrow we strike—yes? Yes. Tomorrow it was.
Around dawn. When it rains.
And suddenly everyone started talking at once.

Some, who had never gone striking before, were shy
and said to themselves: What good can it do?
Some told themselves that Christ, in time, would come
and just as he made bread, make work.
And some were scared or finished with the world.
But when those who were scared, or shy, or sure, were gone,
those who were left went down to sit
all through the night on the beach like one big stone,
without eating, together,
because Daniel said it was best
if everyone dwelt on the matter in hand.
So we sat.

Then, around four, Daniel stood up and said
why we, workless people, were here and on strike.
And how, in two hours time, we would walk
six miles inland and work, for nothing,

all day long repairing the inland road,
without breakfast, leaving our knives behind
in case there was trouble.

Half six. No cockcrow yet. The morning star
half hidden in the rain. We prayed a bit,
and Daniel repeated our reason for striking:
Not as a symbolical, but a normal action.
Not for money, but to show we can work.
And that not to work is a crime against oneself. Yes,
Tuesday we fast, Wednesday we feast off work,
and we moved off, 300 men like an ant
trundling a stone eight times bigger than itself.

One man, a carter, who came from a street
with 30 people in gaol for murder,
and had no good reason to strike except
that his mother insisted, sang:
  O moon, O moon,
  O soldier moon,
  I had rather you at my back tonight
  than the King and all his cavalry.
Which was fine – except there was no moon.

A mile from the beach we split,
going different ways to the place we had chosen,
so as not to disturb the police.

Seven. Less rain. Now and again the sun looks through,
glints off the mattocks as we pile the stones
bigger than melons along the verge, and goes in.
Mud to your knees, but the work goes well;
50 yards cleared in under an hour.
Nine. The sound of lorries on the coastal road.
Will they pass or turn? Will they wait in the village,
or come to us up the inland road.
They turn. They come as near as they can. The police.
700 of them. With guns.

Now the rain has stopped and by ten
we have cleared a little more of the road,

when a fine-boned, short, well-perfumed man,
twirling a little pistol on his forefinger,
stepped down to us and said:
Stop work. I order it. Stop work.
Just stop this work at once. Or else we shoot.

But we did not stop.
Say nothing, Daniel said, and his whisper stood.
Then the well-boned man fired once into the sun,
and Daniel said: We shall sit down and rest.
So all sat down. In mud and wet and cold.
You could see your face in pools.

11am. And the short man said: You see this whistle? Well,
when I have blown it twice you will go home.
Then blew, and blew; then blew, and blew again.
High noon. Mid-air the cuckoo drew a cross
against the soaring lark. Still no one moves.
And so, led by the fine-boned man they pushed
among our faces with their knees
and stood round Daniel, saying: Up. Or else.
And Daniel lay down flat. So it was else.
Pick him up, their leader said, and they, poor chaps,
they tried and tried. But Daniel is six plus,
and, well... not thin; not thin at all; and they,
poor chaps, are not paid much;
and most of that goes on the uniform.
It took seven men who got dirty as hell
to carry him, face downwards, to the truck.

And the charge against him and the rest, was:
Trespassing on public property.
And eight of us (with Daniel and the carter) got
ten years apiece and shared a cell
with eight condemned to death for banditry
watching a pair of cats make love on the roof
while the wireless gave a boxing match.
And over the courthouse porch was carved
    OMNIA VINCIT AMOR
! yes: Don't you fret, the turnkey said,

You're not like them (the bandits). I bet this—
by the time they're shot, you're out.

And a number of famous artists came; wise men,
whom Daniel trusted. And the Communists came,
and made a great to-do up the leg of the land,
and got a Deputy in on the strength of it.
And we got out.

Late autumn. Home. New bread. Good wine.
Better of course than the gaol where old men pine
for the end of their frail, fetid breath.
But the inland road is still a rut,
and half of those who struck went north,
and the fish thieves thieve,
and the red leaves shine so bright
they scorch the wings of passing birds.

The Song of the Imperial Carrion

Not long ago
on the northern shore of the Black Sea
lived many birds and fishermen.
Many birds, but no vultures.

Early one morning
soldiers came.
Brave men led on by gentlemen.
A week — and most lay dead among,
dead birds, dead fishermen.

And before another
week was out,
as if they smelt the English dead
some thousand miles off,
from Africa the vultures came.
Perhaps the wind blew south.

Winter cleaned out
what soldiers there were left.
Only a few
vultures followed the army's ships.
The rest built nests.

So the community of birds
on the northern shore of the Black Sea
increased by one.
And those who go
fishing along that coast today
call that bird the English crow.

As you go to bed
consider the English crow. He flies
like a flag a thousand miles wide
for the soldiers and the fishermen who died
on her majesty's service.

Loyal to the King

Loyal to the king
and to preserve
their nationality,
a tribe of nits
inhabiting
the northern cliff of a turd,
from time to time
made war upon
a neighbouring tribe
over matters of territory.

Often among
the conflicting hosts
tens of thousands
of lives were lost;
sometimes the vanquished were pursued
relentlessly
for up to fifteen days.

Epitaph

I am old.
Nothing interests me now.
Moreover,
I am not very intelligent,
and my ideas
have travelled no further
than my feet.
You ask me:
What is the greatest happiness on earth?
Two things:
changing my mind
as I change a penny for a shilling;
and,
listening to the sound
of a young girl
singing down the road
after she has asked me the way.

A Singing Prayer

I

By mutual fear
we have come in peace
to the end of the year.

Berries gleam
behind green thorns;
and between our smelly frontiers,
fires burn.

Since we began
three full generations of men ago
what has been done about our references
for the time when Christmas comes for us no more?

A dozen wars
count 50 million dead;
not adding on: famine, and plague, and heartbreak.
It is enough to make
the unborn tremble in their wombs.

II

But do not pretend
that the origin of war is mysterious.
Cross-question those who repeat:
Disaster is natural to man.

When you see evil done, do not say:
It is human nature.

Unless when good is done, you say:
It is human nature.

Why imagine
if a thing happens often, it is natural?
Rather
ask after its kind, and where it started.

And do not find
that you cannot be blamed for a thing;
but that you stand against it.

And if you hear:
Why bother us with this? Reply:
Born with strong noses must cry stinking fish.

Shun the household
where questions like these, embarrass...
In the name of gentility
they ask you to button your lip
when faced by evil.

You will, in any case,
not be asked back.
Yet ask your questions, once.
It is little enough; but something; and,
be sure they sleep less tight because you asked.

For the man who is small must think:
Small acts of goodness are no benefit —
and does not do them:
Small acts of malice do no harm —
and does not abstain from them.
Thus he can tell himself:
The river moves the river on.
Combing his hair each day, but not his heart.

Observe the acts of those who claim
to be above such things.

Notice the deeds of who insists
injustice bores her.

And
if you pray,
do not rest content with your prayers.

III

It is hard — I know.
Cold comfort — I know.
And if you came to me you would find
a man needing much forgiveness.

Indeed, I would like to change; to be wise.
And I have been told that wisdom consists
of avoiding strife.
To dig my own square inch till it bears
apples in March, is held to be wise.
Be still, such wisdom says, and when
your neighbour's beard goes up in flames
moisten your own. Make no attempt
to actualise your dreams; but call them vanity,
and lose your shame in compromise.
Alas, I can do none of these things.
It cannot be said that I am wise.

IV

Well over half our century is gone.
We were three generations
possessing opportunity and time
who were too much possessed by them.

Our inheritance contained
much that was wrong;
yet it cannot be said

we were born emptyhanded.

Easily persuaded to slay each other,
among us those who profited from slaughter
lived in peace.
So we made tolerance, a vice.

Infinitely careful of each self,
we stood for liars in public places;
and called it freedom,
because we did not have to hear them.

When you ask after us and find
weakness, falsehood, malice, sin,
and the complex excuses we made about them,
judge us — but with forbearance.

For if we did not seek out
the evil among us too carefully,
nor did we rest in peace.

Take what is best for keeps;
keep what was worst in mind;
for we who measured time by pain
never will return again;
and more than half our time is gone.

V

I wrote this song
for those who will be born
in the time we call New Year,
to be among you there,
even as you are here.

The song is given away
like a man's top-coat when he dies,

who knew it cost too much
for him not meant to last,
and knowing this would make
the same mistake again.

What peace can the living have
when the dead have none?
Agree among you.
Here we three are one.

A Chorus from Antigone

There are many wonders on earth
and the greatest of these is man.
We have divided the world into nations
and we use the land to know
and to nourish ourselves.
Likewise we cross the sea and the changing air
as easily as any room;
even in storms, even at night, for then
we make the white stars guide us through.
Indeed, for man, the dark is brilliant, too!
    Always the first among living things,
beast, bird, or bug, the changing air, or mineral,
we kill, or catch them out,
we mine them with our cunning hands, until
all that is known is made to obey.
    And we have grown inside ourselves,
mind that moves further and faster than light;
and we invented speech
to trap the mind as it flew,
and so to hand things down.
    But even as we make, whatever we make,
and no matter how much we make,
we long to destroy the things we have made.
Finding no enemy, we become our own enemy.
As we trap the beasts, so we trap other men.
But the others strike back, trap closing on trap.
Having eaten enough, man next must build a wall
around whatever food is left,
and other men must pull down that wall.
So the roof gets split;
and the rain and the changing air wash away
whatever is left of man and his cities,
when men have done with them.

1965

I Shall Vote Labour

I shall vote Labour because
  God votes Labour.
I shall vote Labour in order to protect
  the sacred institution of The Family.
I shall vote Labour because
  I am a dog.
I shall vote Labour because Ringo votes Labour.
I shall vote Labour because
  upper-class hoorays annoy me in expensive restaurants.
I shall vote Labour because
  I am on a diet.
I shall vote Labour because if I don't
  somebody else will:
  AND
I shall vote Labour because if one person does it
  everybody will be wanting to do it.
I shall vote Labour because
  my husband looks like Anthony Wedgwood Benn.
I shall vote Labour because I am obedient.
I shall vote Labour because if I do not vote Labour
  my balls will drop off.
I shall vote Labour because
  there are too few cars on the road.
I shall vote Labour because
  Mrs Wilson promised me £5 if I did.
I shall vote Labour because I love
  Look at Life films.
I shall vote Labour because I am
  a hopeless drug addict.
I shall vote Labour because
  I failed to be a dollar millionaire aged three.
I shall vote Labour because Labour will build
  more maximum-security prisons.

I shall vote Labour because I want to shop
  in an all-weather precinct stretching from Yeovil to Glasgow.
I shall vote Labour because I want to rape an air-hostess.
I shall vote Labour because I am a hairdresser.
I shall vote Labour because
  the Queen's stamp collection is the best in the world.
I shall vote Labour because
  deep in my heart
I am a Conservative.

Criminal Incidents

Twilight in autumn. Late birds shake their wings.
Terrorists laugh among the chimneytops.
Yard rises through a skylight. Crack. One drops.
Voices complain about the state of things.

.

Concealed in a bale of dirty sterling
Fred gains admission to the Mint. Midnight.
The watchman masturbates. His memories sing.
Fred's jet-gripped power-drill penetrates the vault
where the coinage dies and the banknote plates are kept.
Yard is in bed. His teeth destroying thieves.
Fred packs his calfskin brief with plates, and leaves.

Beside the park a moonlit constable
asks what the case contains. Is this the end?
Both men are sweating heavily. The Friend
(humming *O Maid of Bangor* by the gate)
wafts the policeman heavenward with his Luger.
He leaves his wife and children to the State.

.

Two men. A corner table at Maxim's.
The eldest thinks grave scenes may well occur
if troublemakers drive Yard's force too far.
Such apprehensions ruin his french beans.
Doubts cloud their tulip glasses; loath to blame
Fred signs the bill with a respected name.

Outside, heroic statues point at Mars.
The Friend is trying doors on family cars.

.

Amplified guitars excite successes;
enthusiasts salute enthusiasts;
flavoured alcohols melt ice; and topless wives
invite adulterous caresses
at the banker's riverside home. Upstairs,
Fred views the family heirlooms with delight.
The Friend keeps watch. Laughter ascends. They leave.
Insurance kisses land by candlelight.

At home, Fred lifts a sherry to his nose.
The Friend corrects his parting in a glass;
then fills his journal as the first birds pass
southward across the Thames, with model prose.

•

Wealthy—the stars they feast, through silk they fart,
then, gone their cash, go poor as when they came.
Police dogs sniff them; shoplifters disdain.
The Friend has squandered everything on Art.

Outside the Church of Mary, Queen of Pain,
small groups of unpaid tradesmen, shout: 'Disburse!'
Humbled by irresponsibility
the Friend attempts to snatch a tourist's purse,
is caught, is held, is: Yard demands a name.
Fred gives him several. Several sleep to die.
They swear: 'A masterstroke, and then—goodbye.'

•

The statues on the Ministry's stone eaves
have massive genitals concealed by leaves.
Two hundred feet beneath this lofty frieze
a line of grousing citizens (so thin
their lice have rickets) wait and wheeze
until the uniformed allow them in.

Nine chimes. Doors yawn. Some nastiness occurs.
It's payday for the old age pensioners.

In Cellar J. Fred whispers to the safe.
It clicks. Alas... he comprehends their gloom.
The Friend relaxes in the boiler room.
His Luger has a tendency to chafe.

Snaffled by Yard, by all abhorred, the throng
give natural justice to such reprobates.
Dying between their fists the Friend donates
his corpse to Science and his mind to Song.
Order restores the other to be shot.   ˙
Blue night. Black day. Ten muzzles lose their dew.
And as the bullets hare towards him, Fred
steps forward, lifts his hat, and says: 'Adieu!'

Gone Ladies

Where in the world is Helen gone,
Whose loveliness demolished Troy?
Where is Salome? Where the wan
Licentious Queen of Avalon?
Who sees My Lady Fontenoy?
And where is Joan, so soldier tall?
And She who bore God's only Boy?
Where is the snow we watched last Fall?

Is Thaïs still? Is Nell? And can
    Stem Héloïse aurene,
Whose so-by-love-enchanted man
Sooner would risk castration than
    Abandon her, be seen?
Who does Sheherazade enthral?
And who, within her arms and small,
    Lies hard by Josephine?

Through what eventless territory
Are Ladies Day and Joplin swept?
What news of Marilyn who crept
Into an endless reverie?
You saw Lucrece? And Jane? And she,
Salvation's ancient blame-it-all,
Delicious Eve? Then answer me:
Where is the snow we watched last Fall?

Girl, never seek to know from me
    Who was the fairest of them all.
What wouldst thou say if I asked thee:
    Where is the snow we watched last Fall?

Letters from an Irishman to a Rat

Dear Rat:
Never until this moment have I met
a so appreciative guest.
Please God, a diet of my old potatoes
does not reduce your sheen.

Dear Rat:
Forgive my carelessness.
The note left (correlative potatoes)
was placed too high.
Of course you could not read it.

Dear Rat:
I fear the worst.
My three disgusting children have acquired
a vicious and emaciated dog.
Suppose it heard your name? –
which is forever on their lips.

Dear Rat:
Greatly to my regret I am not rich.
But have you met my neighbour?
A cloudless squire with six pink children, all
animal mad and more intelligent than mine.
And should you live in his house, dearest Rat,
eight Christians (if we include his wife)
would mention you each evening in their prayers,
whereas at my place there are only five.

New Numbers
1969

This book was written in order to change the world
and published at 12/– (softback), 25/– (hardback), by Cape
of 30 Bedford Square, London, WC1
(a building once occupied by the Russian Embassy)
in 1969.

It is generously scattered with dirty words
particularly on pages 9, 31, 37 and 45,
and was written by © Logue
a sexy young girl living among corrupted villagers
who keeps her innocence through love.
Its weight is 7.926 ounces,
its burning temperature is Fahrenheit 451.
On the day of publication its price would buy
11 cut loaves,
3 yards of dripdry nylon,
5 rounds of M1 carbine ammunition,
or a cheap critic.
What do you expect for 25/–
...Paradise Lost?

This book will offend a number of people;
some of them influential people.
Its commercial potential is slight;
the working classes will ignore it,
the middle classes will not buy it,
the ruling class will bolt it with a smile –
for I am a Western Art Treasure.
What right do I have to complain?
Nobody asked me to write it. Yet,
you may be sure I will complain.

This book is dedicated to new men:
    Astronauts, metermaids, Chinese Ambassadors,
quizmasters, blood-donors, South Vietnamese,
rocket designers, thalidomide babies,
anchormen, skindivers, African Generals,
Israelis and launderette manageresses,

multilingual porpoises, left-wing doctors,
brainwashers, bingoqueens, con
crete poets, pollsters, commuters, computer-
programmers, panels of judges, gas-chamber victims,
abstract expressionist chimpanzees,
surfies and selfmade millionaire teenagers,
skydivers, aquanauts, working-class playwrights,
industrial spies with identikit smiles,
lollipop ladies, and top A'n'R men,
intrusion specialists, and 4-minute-milers,
motivation researchers, and systems analysts,
noise abatement society members,
collective farmers, and war criminals,
transplanted heart men, and waterski champions,
the Misses World, and those I love.

If this book does not change you,
give it no house-space.
If having read it you
are the same person you
were before picking it up —
then throw it away.

Not enough for me
that my poems shine in your eye.
Not enough for me
that they look from your walls,
or lurk on your shelves.
I want my poems to be in your mind:
so you can say them when you are in love,
so you can say them when the plane takes off
and death comes near.

I want my poems to come between
the raised stick, and the cowering back;
I want my poems to become
a weapon in your trembling hands;
a sword whose blade both makes and mirrors change.

But most of all I want my poems sung
unthinkingly between your lips
like air.

Nine completely naked girls
will dance all Sunday afternoon
on the tomb of the Unknown Conscientious Objector.
In keeping with tradition
their profitable mounds will be close shaved;
there will, however, be no posing.
Gooseflesh will rise to sumptuous music,
a medley of Beatle favourites played
by the Foden Motor Works steel band.
At three, a blind war hero,
driven insane by the acid rock,
will leap onto the plinth and scream:
GOD WILL FORGIVE US ALL!
The naked girls will trample him to death.
High in the freezing summer air,
a team of smiling constables will spray
hallucinatory vapours on the crowd
from Red Cross helicopters;
and when these dreamy moistures bead their flesh
troubled enthusiasts will eat each other, raw.
At five, the People's Candidate,
hot from the loss of his deposit in the East,
will seize the microphone. His theme:
Council Housing for Child Murderers – a Beginning.
Next day a racist scholar will demand
increased grants for the parents of the dead.
A spastic faints outside the National Gallery.
Night falls. The sky is full of weeping reds.

Come to the edge.
We might fall.
Come to the edge.
It's too high!
COME TO THE EDGE!
And they came,
and he pushed,
and they flew.

Friday. Wet dusk.
Three blind men outside an Indian restaurant.
They shout at each other.
They have been drinking.

White sticks wave in the doorway.
The place is almost empty.
They feel along the tables.
Two patrons draw their curries back.
They choose a table near the door.
They telescope their sticks.
They wait.

Their order is: two Eggs & Chips, one Curry.
Their chins are up.
Their mouths are slightly open.
One drums the laminated calico.
Their plates arrive.

The tallest of the egg men reads his chips.
He learns their number and their average size.
He who chose curry stirs it, looking upward.

The shorter chip man listens to the tall.
He hears a fork enter a chip.
He hears the chip approach and disappear
forever into his companion's mouth.

And as its mastication starts,
his evil fork moves confidently out
and spears the cluster of remaining chips,
securing two.

He eats them both.
Yolk coagulates on his lapel.
None of them have removed their overcoats.
Shots of the Himalayas line the wall.

The taller's fork returns, touches the plate,
lifts half an inch, lifts, hesitates,
moves to and fro, then stabs the shorter in his face.

All three get to their feet.
The curry man supplies the waiter with his purse.
Their sticks expand. They leave. Outside,
they start to shout obscene remarks.

Madame:
I have sold you —
an electric plug,
an electric torch,
an electric blanket,
an electric bell,
an electric oven,
an electric kettle,
an electric fan,
an electric iron,
an electric drier,
an electric mixer,
an electric washer,
an electric sweeper,
an electric knife,
an electric clock,
an electric fire,

an electric toothbrush,
an electric teapot,
an electric eye,
and electric light —
allow me to sell you,
an electric chair.

Do you see that neat white house
in the middle of its golf-grass lawn?
Day and night the gate is closed.
The owner keeps its realm immaculate
and is herself immaculately clean.
But, thank God, the shit is in her!

A policeman is walking from London to Glasgow.
His handkerchief is wet with tears.
And as he walks, he cries:

I do not want to be cremated when I die.
I do not want to be buried in consecrated ground.
I want to be buried under the M1,
where the traffic never stops,
that those who drive this way can say:
Round about here a policeman is buried.
He died of love.

Three criminals were driving up to town
in a stolen car.
As they passed the policeman the first one shouted:
Goodbye, father!

and the second shouted:
    Goodbye, mother!
and the third one shouted:
    Goodbye, my love!

His case is typical.
On leaving school he showed no tendency to seek
honest employment.
I visited him often.
I formed the opinion that he was not
inherently vicious. However,
during his formative years something had snapped.

He thought everyone was against him.
He took a dislike to his Chaplain.
He failed to draw strength from the Bible.

Though the guards showed him nothing but kindness,
he made no attempt to lighten their task.
He sulked. He was bitter.

And on the last day when the privilege to choose
a reasonable menu is given to those who must die,
he neglected the offer.
He sat saying nothing.

I asked him to listen. I said to him: Lad,
wait till the cyanide egg hits the acid,
then draw a deep breath;
trying to help him in spite of his coldness.

Next day I had a visit from his mother.
You were doing no more than your duty, Governor.

You did your best. You have his mother's thanks.

Your boy was one of my failures, Ma'am.
How could he think the world was against him
with someone like you at his back?

I am studying philosophy.
I do not want to work.
I like to be alone with alcohol.

When the man I lived with left
I never got up before noon.
When the money was finished I used to steal food —
but only luxuries: French pâté. Wine.

I had stolen a jar and two bottles;
I was on my way home to listen to tunes,
and maybe to make
after thinking of what excited me last
myself come, maybe not,
when I saw this boy in the street.

He was little and shy.
He walked like a girl.

Come home with me. Sit there. Open your mouth,
I said.

And when he did I spent the afternoon
pitching my coloured stones into his face.

Not one went in.

He sat so still
He never said a word.
I did not let him touch me.

One year afterwards he phoned.
And after an expensive meal, he said:
    Take this.
A huge watch. Golden as a cross.
    It was my grandfather's.

But I felt sure that he had stolen it.

I think he loved me.

I have to tell you about Mr Valentine.
He was small. Very small. Very clean. Very
shy neat and smiling was he,
Mr Valentine who
spent all of his days
regardless of where he might be,
Topolobambo or Juba or Penge,
looking for someone. His truly. His love.
Very small. Even smaller than he.
Tiny lips tiny teeth tiny breasts tiny feet
mini most mini but perfectly made.

He could not find her.

One day he climbed to the top of a bus;
in London it was, before it blew down;
the upstairs was empty; he chose the back seat;
looking out of the window to find her:

My truly! My truly!
His love.

Up the stairwell came Ruby.
Big Ruby. Huge Ruby. Enormous strong Ruby
with hair on her arse.
She put down her shopping and grabbed Mr Valentine
up by his handstitched lapels and said:

"MINE"

There was no one about.

Ring the bell, Mr V. The next stop is ours.
Where are we going? he wanted to say.
Ring the bell.
And he did.

It stopped. They got off. They walked down the road.
They got married.

Clouds overcame the marvellous sun.

They went to her house. A neat house. A small house.
A house that was meant for a man built like him,
Mr Valentine, but
Ruby was whopping and he was so small
he had to sleep on the crust of the mattress.

Make love to me, Valentine. Kiss me all over,
Ruby would say. And he did.
Make love to me, Valentine. Kiss me all over,
what else could he do?

It was awful. Until
one day as he kissed her and stroked her and licked her
he started a dream.

I am walking through clover, said Valentine, clover,
here is a pathway, there is a tree
with a brook passing by,
and there is a hillside all moony like Palmer,
(see Wordsworth & Wordsworth,
a firm who can do that bit better than me.)

One day by mistake
(except no one makes that kind of mistake)
while walking and dreaming he found it: his ingle.
A place overgrown with odorous plants
that curtain the day with leaves and with flowers,
where a fountain sprang with awakening sounds.
He loved it. He stayed there all day.

Where have you been? said Ruby
big Ruby, fat Ruby.
Oh... nowhere...
Where's *nowhere*?

And each day thereafter he went there alone.

Near to the ingle an Irishman lived.
His name was Red Mick.
Mick's prick was as long as a baby's arm
dangling o'er the side of a pram.
He scared Mr Valentine stiff.

You should meet Ruby.
Whose Ruby?
My Ruby.

That cow with the blubberbub tits?
On the button.
I'd sure like to fuck her.

So when he got home Mr Valentine said:
You are loved.

Big Ruby said nothing.
He's made for you, Ruby.
I know you would like him much better than me.
What's his name?
It is Eire. Incarnadine Eire.
THAT bastard!
Oh Ruby...
NEVER no NEVER,
he's only after one thing.

And just like a woman she stuck to her word.
But wanted to know where Valentine went.

Just you wait by my ingle, dear Mick.
Sooner or later she'll follow. I promise.
O.K.
And she did.

She noticed the pathway. She noticed the tree
with a brook passing by,
and the hillside all moony like Palmer,
and the ingle o'ergrown with odorous plants,
where Valentine went, and she tried to get in.

Mr V. in the foreground.
Come *out* here this instant!
Mr V. stepping backward.
Come *out* here, you schmuck!
as she thrust her head inward.
Another step backward.

Come *out* here!
Come *out* here!
Come —
O, Mr Valentine, help me — I'm stuck!
And she was.

Up strolled Red Eire and lifted her skirt.
You rapist! You monster!
You worse than a beast!
as he skinned off her knickers of dayglow green
I hate you, you bastard!
I hate you! I hate you!
shrieked Ruby, big Ruby, but nobody came.

So Red Mick impaled her; and Valentine kissed her,
and told her old stories, and tickled her chin,
and the fountain sprang with awakening sounds
as water alone can sing in this world.

You bastard! said Ruby, but softer,
You beast...

And Valentine opened her lids and saw mist.

Palmer like moony all hillside;
bypassing brook; there a tree, there a pathway;
late afternoon and they came to her door,
Red Mick and Big Ruby, both living there yet,
they fight, but who cares?

Mr V. felt alone. A bit sad. But amen.
He straightened his tie; Mr Valentine; he;
and started to look for his truly again.

A sergeant of the police
fell madly in love with his daughter,
a girl of fourteen.

All through the summer he lay upstairs
beneath a light blue counterpane.

The heat was terrible.
But the sound of her feet on the lino was worse.

What is the matter with him, dear?
Doesn't he care about you or the Force?
I don't know, mother. I just don't know.

That evening she made him a jelly.
Just as he liked it — with custard; no skin.
Would you like some of this, dear?
Yes. I'd like it.
Let Betty bring it up when she comes in.

It was summer. Late August.
Betty was wearing her gymslip and knickers.
She carried the food on a brown tin tray.

As she came through the bedroom door he grabbed her,
ripped off her knickers,
and fucked her and fucked her until he came,
screaming:

Let punishment come from Above,
for there is none on earth!
Let it fall on my stinking wife!
She is to blame for everything!

Dear Miss Pen:
   I need your help.
I am in love with someone older than myself
(16).
   The trouble is
the boy in question is my sister's love.
   But I can't help myself
when he comes round it hurts so much
just seeing them together.
   But worse than that
I think that he loves me.
He calls me girl; he says my smell is nice;
how nice I dress; and sometimes how
I look so fresh that he could eat me.
   I could go on and on.
What shall I do?
They will be married in the spring,
and it is terrible for me to let her do
something I know she will regret.

He was fat.
He was rich.
He was fifty.

His wife was a drunk.
His son was a junkie.
His daughter went fucking with beatniks.

He flew to Japan in search of tranquillity.

Fuji. Kyoto.
   We have them at home.
Hope would not let him say better.

Going back to the airport the taximan said:
   I know of a place in the north.
   A monastery?

Yes.
Then drive there.

Half a day later:
   Down there.
He paid and walked half a day more.

It was four Nissen huts.
The monks wearing T-shirts.
The abbot was younger than him.

   Sit down.
   Have you found it?
   No.
   Neither have we.

There was nothing to drink except instant.

   These are beautiful cups.
   You may take them.
   Can you get me a dozen?

Brown eyes seeing gray.

   Go two miles further on.
   The factory is there.
   Ask for our man.

He was sitting beside the conveyor.
He was watching the cups go by.
Not taking his eyes off the belt:
   Be seated, he said.
And then,
every so often,
say,
once a week,
he pointed towards a cup going by
and said:
   That one.

Two Lyrics

I

Woke up this morning
in the middle of winter;
salt in my coffee,
sweat in my hair;
the letter said: She's dead,
we know you will miss her.
Woke up this morning
in winter, in winter.

Started my answer,
but failed to remember,
the sound of her voice
or the shape of her head;
wrote I was sorry,
will be there on Thursday;
found myself busy,
sent flowers instead.

Several years later
I saw her when dreaming;
fingernails bitten,
her hands in her hair;
lovely as ever:
I have to get started!
she shouted: *Get started!*
and parted the air.

Woke up this morning
in the middle of winter;
salt in my coffee,
sweat in my hair.
All I could think of
was sleeping beside her;
and how she wore nothing
in winter, in winter.

II

Monday evening;
not much traffic;
leave the car in
automatic;
driving easy,
driving slow,
hearing John on
the radio.

She was lovely,
she was fair;
brightness fell from
her hair;
she was mine but,
as you know,
everybody
has to go.

See the poet.
See him writing.
See the singer.
Hear him sing.
They know nothing
but the moment
when they find the
perfect thing.

She the woman
in her beauty;
brightness falls from
her hair;
she was mine but
time needs filling;
she was mine but,
as you know,
Monday evening,
not much traffic;
everybody
has to go.

Nell's Circular Poem

she came to me in the middle of winter,
two-thirds my age, wearing a furry hat.
When she is happy her smile is like
that of the flower girl who tiptoes up
and down the lawn, and somewhat to the right
of Botticelli's Graces in his *Spring*;
and when she thinks, her upper lip gets thin,
and somewhere inbetween her nose and chin
a delicate obsession floats.
She blinks a-lot. Is punctual. And I love her.

Now it is ten years later to the day.
I answer less. My pubic hair is gray.
And differently I love her more than when

Cats are full of death.
Horses
and even very small dogs
scare me.
I fear I am not very English.

Lately, however,
a mouse has come to live in my flat.
At 40, pushing 41,
a man who lives alone
and breaks his teeth while eating jam
is, is he not,
rather ridiculous?
So I am grateful.

I eat at home more often,
compose with greater ease,
and yesterday I bought a book on mice.

All things considered, he
is very fortunate.
Though poor, I have expensive tastes.
My mouse has camembert and brie in peace,
whereas some mice of my acquaintance run
fantastic risks
for lumps of sweaty cheddar.

I must admit he's not all that intelligent.
The first time I saw him
walking down the middle of the room,
tail in the air —
tra-la!
— I thought he was brave.
Now I realize he had lost his hole.
Later I discovered he had only one eye, and,
needless to say,
posh vets won't have him in their surgeries.
What's more,
Madame won't like him.

But what can you do? —
he has moved in
and she hasn't.

An orange nylon carpet lights their bedroom.
Washable woodgrained wallpaper
associates their parlour with the past.
To dominate the colours of their home
this couple chose as boss hue, frosty mauve.

Why do they view so eagerly tonight?

Two years ago men reached a nearer star.
Near their soft landing visored heroes found
dozing beneath a lucent hibernaculum
a worded creature not unlike themselves.
Re-entry countdown has begun.

Winter has vanished. Spring has gone. The craft is home.
TONIGHT — THE SPEAKING ALIEN WILL APPEAR
ON UPWARDS OF 1000 MILLION SCREENS.
Leaning towards their own, they hear:

> Dearly Beloved, I lack the words to say
> how far away it is, or where it is,
> or what it is we know that you, as yet, do not.
> Bored with the cosy spiral of my galaxy
> I went beyond my failplace and time slammed
> behind me like a door into a pillar box.
> No one I knew could reach that lock.
> But since one missing from the likes of us
> means heavy damages against the rest,
> it was essential to create an instrument
> whereby I could be sprung.
> Therefore we found a vacant paradise
> and broadcast urgent seeds across the third
> and pentecostal satellite of its sun,
> amid whose kindly airs and images
> grave apes could flower as samaritans,
> and fetch me to their earth from whence
> as quick as thought I can reach home.

The screens go white.

O wait for us! O wait for us!
barefooted in the frosty pile they cry.

And coming back across the stars they hear:

    You do not ask enough.
    You only seek the bible of my flight.

    O wait for us! O wait for us! they cry.

She is prepared to leave her antique jar
topped by an adder made of lapis lazuli.

He lived near here.
Before the war most people could not read.

My father came in with the paper
and said: Fetch Mary.

She came in her blue.

    Read it, he said.
She was nine. We had the same stars.

And the article said
how a man had committed the act with his eldest;
and when it was due he took her by tube;
and the hospital was the one facing Parliament;
and on his first visit he grabbed up the child
and ran past the doorman
and down to the river
and threw it right in.

My father gave Mary a penny for reading.

He smoked 40 a day and got killed in the war.

You remember that man they hanged for the drowning?
My mother asked fifteen years later.

Mary had moved. I still have her card.

We knew him.
His wife died of something.
His eldest kept house.
She came here the evening they took him away:

If ever I go to a dance with Yvonne
(the loose one who bit herself off when the Yankees went home)
when I get back he is waiting.
He strips me and has me downstairs.
When he has finished he says:
What you give them—you give me, too.

The funny thing is,
no one had it save him.
Well, maybe a feel—but no more.

I was born on a board;
the central board of a raft.
At five I got a second board;
thicker and stronger than the first.
When I was six I went to school.
I learnt how boards were made.
Twelve years later my name appeared
among those who had passed.
My prize was a board.

Between 18 and 21
I attended university.
I was shown what to do with a board,
and given another to prove I knew it.
My chance had come!
I made my boards into a raft and sailed.
It came apart.
Pushing my boards before me with both hands
I reached the shore, and, finally, the city.
After a week I tried to sell my boards.
No one would buy.
Everyone had at least one board;
and those who needed more lacked means;
and those who had enough refused my price.
They are heavy, I thought. I will give them away.
But those who needed more said I was mad;
and those who had enough said: They are stolen.
They are useless, I thought. I will abandon them.
But those who needed more said: She is treacherous.
And those who had enough confirmed their words.
My chance had gone.
After a time I married a man
with about the same number of boards as me;
and our daughter was born
on the central board of the raft
where we waited together
patiently.

John: who earned his living at sea,
who was as easy at sea as a gull,
feared by the herring, patient with nets,
able to gauge the force of the wind
by its touch on his cheek,

and who knew a few stars well,
lies here.

The sea did not kill him.
He died of age in his daughter's house.
This stone was paid for by his crew.

A Greek who made millions in shipping
is walking alone by the sea.
It is autumn. Near sunset. The wind has died down.
Raising his eyes from his white,
basketweave shoes,
he sees a boat come gliding in
on two bright foils;
its blue patrol-lamp flashing.
And in the wheelhouse of the boat
a man in uniform, reciting,
what the Greek will describe
as a song of great beauty, not sad.

Listen to what the millionaire said:
I will give you the earth if you say it again.
And the man said: I will,
if you sail with me.

In his villa the Greek has a teenage daughter.
Under her sharkskin slacks she is always nude.
At supper her father recounted the incident.
She slept until twelve with her mouth wide open.

Though I gave up an hour ago
my anglepoise continues to fish
my typewriter for the right word.

World famous and effective bomb,
you burst like lux,
and your voice resembles the sound of a weir
heard from far off on a winter morning.

Holy and gorgeous is the cloud that hangs
in frosty air above Sin'kiang.
Dust falls as quietly as snow
falls from the blue bamboo leaf, onto snow.

My grandfather turns in his sleep and says:
There are guests at the door. Receive them kindly.
Sleep tight, old man, I say.
It is nothing. Tomorrow will be fine.

When I was serving my country
a staff-sergeant said:

    There's dozens of ways, but if everything fails
    put your head on her shoulder
    your prick in her hand,
    and cry.

He slept on the bunk above me in Wrexham,

and what he said was true.

    Christ,
said the boy who got into Airborne
and died outside Caen,
    when you're coming you wish your pipe was a mile long.

His hair was yellow. He came from Stroud.
And what he said was true.

On the way to Port Said they showed me a photo;
an overhead take from the side of a troopship
moored in the roads of Singapore harbour.
On the water below us,
a two-eyed bumboat heaped with souvenirs;
and in its bows a woman, naked, arms upspread,
holding the seamed edge of a muslin sheet
that billowed outwards from her hands, and tugged
against the regulation belt strapped round her hips.

    I am for sale, too!
they cried she cried.
She must be dead by now.
And I am sure that what she cried was true.

Why do you like it in England, scout?
You get a good smoke for 50p
and there aren't too many niggers about.

Caption for a Photograph of Four Organised Criminals

This is the final statement we shall make:
Although we got no less than we were due,
pity the likes of us, and God may take
pity, my friends, upon the likes of you.
Observe us in the middle of the air;
four rashers off a putrid barbecue;
the stink alone is half enough to scare
you out of all the wrongs you long to do.
So get down on your honest knees and swear:
Be good to us — and we'll be true to You.

Your kids became our addicts, and our whores;
we broke your strikes; and, when the need arose,
we bought your officers, we bent your laws,
how many witnesses we slew, God knows —
you stupid, vain, selfrighteous, ugly bores! —
we, the dynamic impresarios
who gratified your soft, incarnate flaws.
If you should feel some recompense is due,
mention us when you make that deal of yours:
Be good to us — and we'll be true to You.

Gas, gunshot, Alcatraz, the electric chair —
only the best machinery could do
justice to the exuberant despair
you legal felt for us illegal few.
Please do not let such absolutions stun
your dreaming hearts; it is high time you knew,
from Paradise to Pandemonium
there's but one make of different men, not two,
crying outside the gates of kingdom come:
Be good to us — and we'll be true to You.

Remember this, good men who passed your time

securely chained while squealing to be free:
Without society there is no crime,
and without crime there's no society.

Winter 1968

How can I help the revolution?
What do you do?
I am a poet.
I understand. I used to be a poet, too.

One evening my husband came home
and said he had been to a prostitute.
He had been drinking with friends.
They went to a strip-club and then,
one thing led to another and then,
they visited this lady.
I tried very hard to forget it.
I did all I could to forget it.
I said time would help me forget it.
But I could not forget it.
Six months later I started proceedings.

The police have been keeping close watch
on the beatnik community.

They have raided several derelict houses
searching for clues.

In the suburbs an old woman has drawn out her savings.

Only two fine weeks that summer.
Army recruiting went badly.
Five soldiers were killed while patrolling in Aden.
And a beatnik girl was found battered to death
in a derelict house near the gasworks.

Dear Mother...

There were troops in the dunes.
You could see them muttering words into sets,
learning to pacify trouble spots, yes,
but the girls in bikinis disgraced it.

The news came by wire.

The last time they saw her the beatnik was wearing
a dipaway blouse in dovecoloured hopsack.

We deeply regret...

During the season at Folkestone they keep
the gentlemen's lavatory open all night.
In the twilight world of drugging and sex,
you can never tell when something might happen.

She is going to buy a ticket to Aden.

Each morning you see them, respectable men
washing under their arms; they don't care.
Almost total strangers use the same flannel.

For Aden?
Yes, Aden.

Although she worked hard for her levels

a nice girl has gone with the beatniks.

Why on earth is she going to Aden?
God knows. Did you let Simon do it?

Hawks upon cadges. The women unclean.

I was scared.
You scared?
To get out of his car.
£275. You pay over there.
I haven't done it with anyone either;
not since that girl near the waxworks.

The Colonel received her the evening she landed:
Very well. But I'm strongly against it.

But I promised him Saturday night.
You mean you don't want it?

The Ruler receives them.
His carpet is spattered with hawk mutes.

What does this infidel woman want?

The police have no answer. The file stays open.

She would like to see her son's grave.

He watches her fingers. The black plastic handbag.

No news for a year, then the file will close.

Next morning the Ruler showed her the derricks:
We have terrible people in our country, too.

Neither she nor her son will be heard of again.

During her first three months at Norten Art School
she has been singing with the local group.
Her song: *Don't Let Me Go*.
Before she left two 3rd year students fucked her.

She has been interviewed:
"I have been singing all my life."
The hotel bedroom overlooks the sea.

Her first big song: *True Love*.
The man who wrote it had her on the bed.
"Make sure your manager is queer," he said.
He liked the dog-and-bitch position best.
The flip side was called *Sleep*.

"Her image must be linked with joy and hope;
with youthful aspiration." She has signed.
Her sister liked him better than the rest.
"I have to urge her all the time.
Sometimes I let her know that I am pleased."

Her first LP: *Love Is My World*.
Her photograph: Returning from a holiday in Greece.
Her clothes: Silvered trapeze, chrome twill, gray foulard
  smock.
Her weight:
Her car:
Her age:

"For God's sake marry me!"

Two films: **Drum City, Everything in Time.**
Drum City Girl is her first gold.

She buys her parents a dream bungalow.
He liked the dog-and-bitch position best.

"Sometimes I let her know that I am pleased."
Her nickname has become a household word.
Her weight. Her car. Her photograph. Her age.

Fucked up the arse while touring America,
polaroid snapshots of her being licked
are circulated in chic discotheques.

Then:

Mountains seen through rain and cloud.
The wall is high; the house,
a glassy smudge between the foliage.
Sometimes the tourists who walk
along the footpath of the lower slope,
notice a rubber hand pull down a blind.
Needles are hovering in the private room
where she has come to rest.

She has a dog, dark glasses, and a book.
Now and again a plane flies overhead.
35 miles to the west,
her money blossoms in a numbered vault.
When she returns she will be asked:

"What are your views about religion?"
And she will say:
"If God is love, then I believe in God."

He was a youth from the suburbs.
He was very goodlooking.
His father supplied him with money.
His mother was proud.

He was all a young man from the suburbs should be.
But love had it in for him.

Sure as the precipices fall
downwards from Madagascar through the blue,
then indigo, then lightless fathoms of the sea
until they fan into abyssal plains
stretching between Mauritius and Ceylon,
he fell as their eyes crossed.

I have used love like a dog.
Hearing of men who lurked for days
outside a certain person's flat,
afraid to ring the bell,
I grinned.

And now I think I see her in the street;
and now I know the way she holds her head;
and feel as if we've known each other years.

    Come up.

    I love you.
    Do sit down.
    I love you.
    Would you like a drink?
    I love you.
    You know lots of girls.
    I love you.
    What a thing to say.
    I love you.
    No? A man like you?

Tucking her feet up under her bum.

    I think I see you in the street.

I know the way you hold your head.
I feel we've known each other years.

Putting her feet down. Seeing her toes.

   I cannot love you back.
   I have a man. He sleeps with me.
   He's kind. He treats me well.

And so he should!

A fly wrings its hands on the rim of his glass.

And as they sat not talking
thinking
what can he be/she be thinking,
off of his wrist he slipped the leafy watch
along whose strap gold periwinkles had been stitched
in Paris, France,
and hid it in the chair,
and left.

Late sun behind dense cloud makes daylight neon.

She is washing her hair.
She is stripped to the waist.
Her nipples are soapy.

   Where has he gone?
   In spite of his words
   he wasn't slow to be off.
   But no one else has said such things.

Now she is nude as a needle and looking
for something translucent and long

through whose black webs her knees can gleam.

Some music while I do my eyes.

Drum City Girl

His watch.

"Tell him his watch is safe,
and if he wants it he can pick it up."

We see them by an ornamental lake.
Now and again a plane flies overhead.
Some eighteen inches separate their lips.

I do not want the watch.
I owe you nothing. Nor you me.
A pause.
Doesn't it hurt to beat your head this way?
Another pause.
Well?
Pause. Pause.
Please take it back and let me go.
And so he took it from her hand.

Then, in the water, where her face
lay fractionally beneath the lens
where air and liquid meet,
he pitched the automatic gem, and said:

Lucky for her you do not want it, love.
I'm sure that she would thank us both
if water had a door.

And hearing this her mind withdrew from other things
and let his trueness rise into her heart
and cast her eyes in his
and arms in his
and kissed his kiss

and other things
not to be mentioned in a book like this.

They said: The pilot overshot.
They said: It was a holiday tragedy.
They said: The names of those who died
will be withheld until the relatives have been informed.
They said: we need a piece about the relatives.
They said: the one to get is Mrs J.,
young, lost her husband and two kids,
they said that she lives here
a glass front door set in a painted wooden frame
left slightly open, I go in.
The radio is on.
I have to shout hello quite loud
before she says: Come up.
She's on the bed, half drunk,
with new clothes strewn all over.

You're from the women's paper, I suppose?
You want to know exactly how I feel about the crash?
Well this is how I feel:
I'm glad he died. I'm glad.
He hadn't touched me for three years.
As for his dirty kids, I hated them.
I'm glad they're dead and I've still got my looks,
and £20000.

Backed by six blacks,
a girl whose voice makes English sound Chinese,
croons through the speakers of a moonlit room
32 floors above North Street.

The apartment is spotless.
Lit by a tilting lamp
its tenant stiffens in a leather chair.
Five hours ago at 30000 feet
he saw the sun
and took its photograph.

Worth above seven figures when last sold,
spotlit within its alcove,
stands his urn.

O come all ye faithful
here is our cause,
all dreams are one dream,
all wars civil wars.

Lovers have never found
agony strange;
we who hate change survive
only through change.

Those who are sure of love
do not complain,
for sure of love is sure
love comes again.

.   .   .

The Girls

By the weir it says: DANGER.
Chromium fittings wink from the opposite bank.

I can borrow his car. Are you on?

Sun like ripe tungsten edged with wax polish;
and in the middle air,
gliders discover mosque-coloured thermals
on a day when sunlight makes water taste dry.

I have something to tell you. A secret.

NO COACHES

She sees far too much of that girl.

And her grandmother said:

You can never be sure when something will happen.

You drive.
Will he mind?
It is low as a toy.
Will he know?

The fake hide is hot and slightly adhesive.
It sears her
Hang on!
while she braces, then
Better?

You bet.
and they go.

Silk,
blotting the small of her back;
on the lip of the coachwork, her forearm,
palm half raised, digits parted for cooling;
a chill, flowered sweat in each fork.

You had something to tell me? A secret?
For later.
They are really quite close. But nothing has happened.
We might get a boat.
Can you row?

The driver nods. Her shoes are off.
Streaks of dark crud between her toes.
Ask how she drives, she answers: Fast and safe.

Those fucking morons in their caravans!

and many would be pleased to see her trashed.

You like my hair this way?
Clean bands of wand mascara guard each lid.
You like it long?
Edges and scents divide her from the world.
Perhaps it needs a cut.
Next left.

So brightly the sun between leaves
they seem black. Gates painted green,
other cars   other cars,
and between them the white, misty wealth
of homes set on golf-grass, well back from the road,
NO COACHES   NO COACHES   NO COACHES

and where, to the right, behind elm trees, the sky
leaps upward from the river's diamond head,
sunbeams prosper on hand-stitched surfaces,
oval enlargements glide over linen,
they park.

Cash. Cap.
  I have your bag.
Doors thock. Thighs glare through cotton filters.
Eyes abound.
  You keep the key.
They wade through chrome.

"WHEN GOD SAYS YES — SAY YES TO GOD"

Leaves mute the weir. Its waters sound
like cola seething in a paper cup,
mixed with a choir that sings through tiny grilles:
  '*It is not dying,*
  It is not dying.'

  I could do with a lolly.
  Get two — then wait beside the boats.
They part.

The driver bobs; three boating oafs
enjoy a dirty joke; she says: Which way to find the boats? —
and bobs (someone would like to punish her in silk)
along the slatted catwalk to the brink.

Some 50 yards north west,
a queue for *Mr Softee*.

Purse in her hand
pin in her mouth
head to one side
squeaky clean hair leaning out —

does the comb leave red tracks?
does her scalp like the feel of its teeth?
Rubber snaps.

Behind her in the queue a man in serge
his inside pocket filled with naked prints.
And as she peels the ice,
and as the feasting surface of her tongue
flickers along its smoky pole
—O, he could take such shots of it,
—shots called: I love your tongue,
I love its tip, O office butterfly!

She fears his grip. She needs her friend. She goes,
quickly towards the river's brink,
and ivies lick her cheeks like tiny fish.
Weeks later in a crowded auditorium
masked by the cheering voices his will shriek:
SUCK THIS—YOU FUCKSOME BITCH! SUCK THIS!
and as the anthem fans their politics:
BITCH! BITCH! BITCH! BITCH!
and then she hears his vicar's sandal creak,
and as she runs toward her friend,
and as her friend's well-bitten fingertips
dandle her frightened scents from bank to peak,
triangles blind his lens,
and laughter stripes his mind;
and as her friend unties
and as she hops the peak
and as they glide away, away, she stoops
letting her panties smile:
    "Goodbye to him."

Seen by an airborne eye, beyond the weir
the aimless river glitters between miles

of almost empty, almost silent green.
A towpath blurred by spreads of August vetch
doubles its northern bank; and here and there,
a millimetre-furlong from the brink,
houses half-thought, half-seen among their leaves;
blue syrup air, so still, so still;
and on the river's eastward gliding width,
the boat; and far beyond, imagined more than seen,
the shimmering estuary.

Water; spring water; is lucid; bends sunlight;
strongly it mirrors; substances change in its hand.

Images; skylit; flowing through images;
lips hanging open; hooks lancing succulent membranes;
breasts fenced by wire meshes;
well-sharpened nipples stuck through; seeking teeth.

Three miles downstream from where we saw them last
a boy has risen from his bed,
taken his sub-machine-gun from its box,
pulled on his shirt and gone
to the stable with sleep in his eyes.

The water flows east; she is rowing; she thrusts;
white straps dangle latches; opulent flesh wells over elastic;
and the one they call pretty just sprawls
saying nothing, but nothing, her eyes saying nothing;
and behind them the sound of the weir fades to nothing;
and above them the noise of a plane no one sees.

Cut to the boy: he cinches; he mounts;
behind him the house is asleep under shutters.
He is nine; about nine; he knows the horse well.
How it stops; how it stands to the gate; and how,

as he touches the latch with his toe,
it sniffs, passes through, and turns west on the towpath.

Is somebody calling?

Blade water light beneath blade's metal tip.
Water evolving dark whorls in their wake.
Oars easily buried, length bent by the light,
pulled through the water's continual door
by her body's soft lever. Up, into sunlight
it rises; she rises; eyes pour over fists into eyes,
as the varnished prow splits miraculous dust
on the other girl's insteps, her thighs,
as she curves in the heat amid pillows.

The sun has moved west. It aims at the boy.
See the gun on his knees. See the horse,
how it steps through the nettles.

Is somebody calling?

And the sky is an empty blue jar;
and the high, wooden strakes of their fortress touch heaven.
And aside from the light
occasional drip of an oar, all is silent;
she slips them, and glides from her blouse:

I'm so hot.
So am I.

and glides from her blouse. How whitely they shudder!—
though the world sees no more than an elbow—
they drift.

You had something to tell me? A secret?

on the curve of her pupil the other girl's lips

Last night I was tired. Dead tired.

But sleep never came.

her fingers unlocking a column of teeth

I got up.
I was naked and sweaty.

I went to the kitchen.

there are leaves on the water

Go on.

And when I came up—
From the kitchen?
—the kitchen

the leaves on the water

his door was half open.

her father's

He sleeps on his own.
It's years since he touched her.

her mother

Go on.

see the leaves on the water

He was sleeping on top of the clothes.
I went in. With the milk in my hand.
Something pushed me.

leaves high on the water

I looked at his... I—
don't hate me, don't hate me,

I wanted to —
Tell me. I love you. Please tell me.
I wanted to —

all of a sudden

And did you? And did you?

all of a sudden they twirl through the reeds
and vanish away.

The gun is elegant.

Born to the meditations of a man
who lived between the wars in Germany,
its moving surfaces required exactitude
measured to tens of thousandths of an inch
before the boy on indoor days could watch
the apparition of his vacant face
hover beneath its oily sheen.
And when he practises all afternoon
down in the fainting meadows by the weir,
he aims into the blaze and knows the snout
no hand can match for rapid punishment
is baffled.

And did you? And did you?

Blood tests do not reveal the past.
Much of his parents' time is spent abroad.
But in the house with shutters always closed
a woman called Lacksheesh
feeds him, and cuts his fingernails, and sings;
and almost all their cash (that comes by post)
is spent on ammunition, scotch, and hay.

Immovable heat. The water is foil. Wing becomes leaf.

Insects are gemstone. He enters their circle.

    I love you.
    I love you.

    Is somebody calling?

no sound from the earth and the light is like oil

    I love you.
    I love you.

his ears mark the source, he rides forward,

    I love you.
    I love you.

they say.

And the reeds smell of autumn already;
and the water between them is still.
And the reeds stretching down through the water;
its stillness, their stillness, repeating
shots of his father's tall-faced horse
with the rushes piercing its neck.

Advancing kisses thread the image of her body
to their tip. Suspended on that tip, her scents,
her coloured textures, day, and age, are weightless names
flicked backwards into nothingness away;
and as the sunlight mutters in her throat,
her spine's arched lance
presents its centre to the vivid bud.

The boy sees fish: innumerable fish
crushed by the surface as their moat is drained.
Fishes that boil and suffocate, that dive through fish;
fish wallowing on fish, with other fishes kicking in their jaws;

the slap of desperate fish that half rise up,
and up, as if to pitch their loathsome effluent
over the riverbank and him.
The gun keeps time.
Echoes that question the daylight's priority
flee under miles of greenish cloud
toward the known world's end;
and as the bullets squeeze into the light,
their leader sends the first
of many cone-shaped waves across the air;
and through that funnel apex after apex drifts
aimlessly on towards the missing girls.

The sky begins to fall. Thick drops, and slow,
round, heavy, sensual drops; fat drops
that waver in the quietude, that pause
a moment, pause a moment, pause, and then
divide into that kind of hammering rain
old men forget until the end of their reunion.
Tree crests explode; the river's surface smokes,
so wedded to the air you cannot see
the child urge his horse across the stippled brink.

Widespread upon the river's cloudy fall,
heavy as white, wet, winestained bread they lie.
And though the smudge they make is lost in rain,
and clouds, divided by long vents of slating gray,
reflect that time when late birds swoop in threes
towards the fading image of the hills,
the boy can see their fingers, beckoning;
and, as the horse turns back, can hear his name
lovingly called by those who lead the way.

Late on the kind of summer afternoon
when intermittent rain has kept us in,

the sky is sometimes emptied from above,
and, hoping to catch an hour in the sun,
until we reach the open fail to see
the day has entered into evening while we sat.
Reaching the bank we find the river full;
broader than we remembered it; quite still.
The land is there to frame the estuary.
The estuary to underwrite the sky.
Everything makes us certain night will fall
without a sign of life on either hand:
and we are on the point of leaving, when,
just for an instant something emerald flares
among the crosslights rising off the sea
and exits through the seamless curvature
of water mixed with sky and quiet stars.

The Isles of Jessamy

'Twas on the good ship Dollymop
the crew made no attempt to stop
their Captain drinking hypnopop —
   known as *The Mermaid's Tea.*

He climbed the mast and shouted: "Mark
leewards the highbrowed Cutty Sark!
Quiet as the fin of a tiger shark
   she parts the sunlit sea."

"Do not mislead us with your woe
dear Captain," sighed the Mate, "we know
the little shirt you mention-o"
   (the crew wept openly)

"went down a thousand days ago.
Each witch-prowed stitch of calico
and all aboard her lie below
   the Isles of Jessamy."

Out from the mast the Captain drew;
then doffed his bowler as he flew.
Over the white horizon's blue
   they heard his: "Goodbyeee..."

Whenceforth his seamen trace the lanes
that slate the great abyssal plains
where none may stay until he gains
   the Isles of Jessamy.

Fragment

It is time I got out.
It is time that I left this city.
For years I have quarrelled with everyone;
I wrote malicious things because
inflicting pain was agreeable
and the pay quite good;
often as not the things I wrote
were stolen from better writers than me,
though sometimes lesser men served just as well.
Be that as it may; it is time I got out;
but I hate the countryside,
and the peasants scare me.

May the 14th
and a letter comes from my mother, saying:
I went down to the hospital
and all they said was, well,
reaching your age our aches will be the same.
So that is that. I cannot knit.

53 years I have been in your city
and still I do not know you or your ways.
I talk too much; and when I talk
gesticulate too much; and slender booms
endlessly tending cinderbeds along the city's cut
affect me deeply.

What am I doing here, anyway?
After 53 years I represent no one;
I give no comfort; I produce no change.
No clamour of a common weal or woe
summons the lesser clamour of my tongue
to give its resolution clarity.

As for the part of shouting evil down,
my need of it is fading as the light
around the house that hides my failing fades
a little earlier each day as winter comes.

October. Late birds shake their wings.
There is a certain brightness in the air:
for those who wish to turn new minds to heaven
and not deny their ancestors, it says;
that general celebration must fulfil
the perfect wording given to me by those
who wave from their allotments as the train goes by.

Words. Open words. Closed words.
Shouts from a passing window. Things
wives hear about soon after lighting up.

I have no taste for everlasting truth;
and they have other fish to fry.

25,609
miles on the clock of my car.
Tomorrow is a mystery.
The past moves quietly away.
no one is asking me to stay;
and yet I do not go.

Besides, where should I go?
My skin is white. My one good eye, is blue.
With these most grievous signs against my kin
the time on earth still left to me
will pass explaining things away
that cannot be explained away.
Of course, I might pretend to be a Jew:
no, no – the risk is still too great –
as the rain rises on the dawn wind
and the gulls stall over Lambeth, where,

flat as a plank split by the sun's meridian,
the river spills bright sheaves of water
on dependent sheaves,
until the lighted estuary streams up the sky.

One evening, through the windows of a house
whose garden trespasses on Primrose Hill,
I saw a man in general's uniform
seated before a table spread with maps.
He had the dreamy gaze of one who'd crossed
the cinder basins of a planet where
sublime attempts were made to ruin war,
and now the given bearings of that march
bisect his waist (and he has double checked them, carefully)
realises he has lost his cavalcade;
his men, his wife, his child, his horse, his dog,
and finally, his reason.

Filled with tears
to see this brave old man so troubled in the dusk,
I knocked, pointed towards the latch, and said:
before my words were out he drew the blind.

Blue light through pleached green.
Only the faraway race of an adding machine
through the architect-crafted factory's half
opened office block window today
being Sunday.

Silence that man.
How dare he call my idleness to mind.
Is it not half enough that all the world
sits hang hand idle on a day like this?
How it deprives my pleasure of its sting
knowing that all are idle, all;

licking each other's parts, no doubt;
thoughtful; beside themselves to be
also getaway sunfunsters.

   Perhaps the man is clever?
Dare I drift tiptoe in some poolside thing,
and, where the outfall slides
over the trouty footage of the weir,
call out: "I say —
three times as much as you are getting now
to follow me."

   Time flies.
Bats dip their wingtips in the starlit pool.
My towel stays moist.

   How I detest this planet!
Fifteen governments have failed
to crown my head.
Despite my hangdog charm, my silver wit,
my small, consoling pout,
I compose these exquisite sentences
in clothes that are almost threadbare.
I have done my best to explain.
I have said:
I only wanted to get my name in the papers.
When nobody put my name in the papers
I refused to complain, I was patient.
But now that I cannot afford the papers
and have to rely on my landlord for news,
my hope is most immeasurably low. My tears
fall quietly as hair
falls from a comb into the goose-necked pan.
Who will look after you when I have gone,
my verses?
Who will there be to like you when I make
that instant hole?

   The car arrives. I tell the driver: "Jane,
we may fly home tomorrow. Hold the plane."

Duet for Mole and Worm

"Kindly do," said the Mole,
"not obstruct the Public Hole."
"Forgive me," said the Worm, "for being blind."

"You will find," said the Mole,
"(if you practise self control)
the lack will not debilitate your mind."

"But my mind," cried the Worm,
"(as my parents will confirm)
is squeeze'n'squirm anoptically combined."

"Yet designed," said the Mole,
"for a Great Symbolic Role."
"Do you think so, Mole?" said Worm. "How very
    kind."

Ch: "Freeze the lake! Frost the grass!
Through the Underworld we pass,
a-busy-be-low-burrow-iggl-kin!"
"You know," said the Mole, "where you are – in a hole:
if you do not meet each other coming out,
you are sure to meet each other going in."

(*They strut*)

M: "How pitiful, dear Worm, to be a human..."
W: "Creation's only wrinkle, Mole! Poor man..."
M: "Imagine every day bar one day Monday..."
W: "Part beef, part bluff, part pique, part marzipan..."

Ch: "Me the First! PhD!
Failed to make it in a tree!
While-we-go-busy-borrow-iggl-kin!"
"You know," said the Mole, "where you are – in a hole:
if you do not meet each other coming out,
you are sure to meet each other going in."

Singles
1973

I

"What have you got at the top of your legs?"
　　"Nothing to do with you.
What have you got at the top of your own?"
　　"Practically nothing, too."

"Give me a look, give me a look,
I have a need to know
Where I came from just as much
As where I am going to go."

II Chinese England

Hilltops seen through rain and cloud.
On his way home the angler feels
the weight of his clothes.

III

Last night in Notting Hill
I saw Blake passing by
who saw Ezekiel
airborne in Peckham Rye.

IV Landscape

The house where we live is white and low;
built by a man who came for the money,
it stands looking south over hills that flow
into hills of a darker green, creased, east
to west by the loops of a shimmering river
greatly attractive to mist;
and sometimes the mist comes as high as the house,
and my room seems to float among leafy domes,
and somewhere behind us a spring has been rising
between two limestone posts
for more than a thousand years,
and the man is buried.

V

Travellers sometimes return.
Flying from London to Paris today
I thought of Tu Fu
going by boat from Chang Lin to Way So
(where he lost all his teeth) in 767.
And I thought: his trip was forever;
and how, if I get there on time,
forever for me will also be long.

VI To the Moon

Self made Moon,
aurene Selene,
favourite address of my heart!

VII Hopeful Ignorance

Flushing a library replete
with famous books I have not read
depresses me.
Dusting my shelf today I bred
that void again.

VIII In the Restaurant

"Snow on toast?"
"Two snows on toast."
"No snow on toast."

IX Layabout

On days when I intend to work
I clean my room as if I were
expecting an important guest.
That done, I sit and ask myself:
  what can have kept her?

X Selfrighteous Rhyme

O Wystan Hugh, you told a lie:
it is not or, but and and die.

XI To a Friend in Search of Rural Seclusion

When all else fails,
  try Wales.

XII

I am wanted for murder in a neighbouring country.
A man in a straw hat rowed me ashore.
Next day I betrayed him and joined the police.
Do not ask for my number. Do not ask me to stay.
It is words that deceive me. Your words.

Mixed Rushes
1974

I

I like this place. The sky is clear.
The wind is ferried over by that hill.
Yesterday afternoon I met a girl.
She had good legs.
The kind that do not meet until the crotch.
Her bride-price was ten thousand pounds.
Time to move on.

II

Pin this to your wall.
Then,
though you have no love for me,
my writing can admire your breasts.

III

Her body makes me grateful to nature,
and mindful of my own.
Her word part, her dumb part,
both delight me;
lightly I touch her half parted lips
with the tip of my tongue.

IV

If the nightflights keep you awake
I will call London Airport and tell them
to land their dangerous junk elsewhere.

And if you fall asleep with the sleeve
of my jacket under your head,
sooner than wake you, I'll cut it off.

But if you say:
"Fix me a plug on this mixer,"
I grumble and take my time.

V

Who knows when love has had its day,
Who never leaves can never say,
For can who cannot please today
Say: "Yesterday I did?" —
When I who can is but who may
Be sure what now does not gainsay
Tomorrow shall forbid?

VI

She has not crossed my mind for years;
and yet,
seeing her name in an old address book,
I flinch.

VII

Last night in London Airport
I saw a wooden bin
labelled UNWANTED LITERATURE
IS TO BE PLACED HEREIN.
So I wrote a poem
and popped it in.

VIII

Where are you going?
Down the road.
What to do?
To change the world.
Why do you want to change the world?
Because I cannot change alone.

IX

I was lying in bed when I noticed
my Tetrastigma looked thirsty.
After awhile I got up and gave it a drink.
Then I went back to bed and watched it:
closely.
Some ten minutes later it gulped
and grew 3/64ths of an inch.

X

"False friend," cries the dying lily,
"now all you think of is Campanula."
"Lily," I sigh,
"who smelt as good to every passer-by,
you will have trumpets plus when I
perennially am granular."

XI

Heart, shaped like a plantain leaf
seen from above,
would you were still as green!

From Abecedary
1977

A

Two big blacks on a 15 bus,
Ali For King their quid pro quo:
"He may be quick — but is he strong?"
"Is Ali *strong?* O, daddy-o,
When that Mohammed pats your cheek
It breaks your little toe."

B

Hermes streaked to Olympus and said:
"The Humans are avid for war."
"Not that business at Troy all over again?"
Said the Beard. "What a bore... what a terrible bore."
And Jetankle whispered: "Not Troy —
This time they want Paradise Coast."
"They are coming for Us?"
"They are coming for Us —
And Boney is lording their host."

E

Einstein received a questionnaire
Whose poser begged him to declare
Whether he thought we might be forced
Into atomic holocaust.
And turning from his triple chess
The figured wizard thereanent
Wrote: *Yes — but not by Accident.*

H

From Hitler's stone scrub Hitler's name,
But let the epitaph remain:
HERE LIES A MAN WHO HATED MEN
And underneath maintain:
WE WISH HIS MUM HAD FELT THE SAME

J: James Joyce

'Tis just as well
In the Customs shed
They search my bag
But not my head.

L

Da Vinci gained a brilliant start;
He had no need of rhyme or rule;
At 10 he broke his mother's heart;
No doubt the woman was a fool.

For likely students he'd provide
A so definitive critique,
Several committed suicide;
No doubt the wretched boys were weak.

And when his sister wrote to say
"My man is dead and we are four,"
He answered: "Give the brats away."
No doubt her youngsters were a bore.

Yet when doubt's done all doubting can,
There is, alas, no doubting it:
Da Vinci was a superman,
And Leonardo was a shit.

M

Marx emerged from a Pullman compartment
And said unto Engels: "I thirst."
"With the ticket you chose," Engels said, "I propose
The last of my Château d'Aumerst."
Said Marx: "Don't be mobbish. We seek to abolish
The third class, not the first."

S

"Indeed, de Sade," snapped Marat, "you will bring
Suspicion on your blest integrity.
Why hesitate to execute the King
Yet claim to be
Revolted Atheistical, like me?"
"You miss my point, Jean Paul," the Marquis said.
"Whilst thinking like a Revolutionary,
I do not give a damn about his head.
However, as an Atheist, I see,
If Christ had died of piles, and in bed,
It might have finished Christianity."

V

Expostulating nose to nose
Down by the ancient Seine,
Victor Hugo roared: "Write prose
And save *La France*, Verlaine!"

"Hugo!" the poet cried, "you're right...
My prose would save the State!
But O my hand could never write:
On Thursday evening Fred was late."

Z

"Zoroaster is the name
For my new horse," said Lady Jane.
"Indeed," her khanji said, "that's odd —
My wife calls her donkey, God."

The Crocodile

(After Peter Nickl)

Beneath a palm, beside the Nile,
a viridescent crocodile
relinquished 40 winks,

to heed a brace of divorcees
engrossed by their accessories
before an ancient sphinx.

And in the twinkling of an eye
the requisites such ladies buy
became his Apogee;

and when they swore the cream were kept
"In *Krokodil*, in France," he leapt,
without a bent rupee,

aboard abaft a mite caïque
that wafted aft a like caïque
that waft towards the sea.

A crocodile can shoot the Nile
as quickly as a mouse an aisle;
but France lies far away...

Where (on-and-with) a Pharian air
he charmed a passing millionaire
to yacht him to Marseilles.

What toothsome scraps! what snacks galore!

missed from the train that northward bore
him to the home of chic.

"Paris betimes," the reptile thought;
and in a café, ere he sought
the sleekest of the sleek,

akimbo legged he called: "Au lait —"
and sipped and saw to his dismay,
   the custom swoon,
   the waiter freak,
   the boulevard grown dumb.

"What ails the brilliant, pale baboon,
to quake before a pilgrim come
3000 miles to seek

his moon, his mosque, his plume, his plum,
that fabulous emporium,
The Crocodile Boutique?"

But when, alas, he stepped inside,
"O hateful Mastermind!" he cried,
(while tears illume his cheek),

"Amongst these lavish odds and ends,
behold — the remnant of my friends!"
(then yawns his emerald beak),

"Shop-girl, beware. Your flesh is frail.
My cousin Salamander's tail
might swinge its winsome pulp.

Therefore protected thou shalt go

in crocodile from tip to toe – "
(and downed her at a gulp!)

And thus to drink the Lotus flood
and lollop thorough Pharaoh's mud,
southward he went that day.

The shop-girl's bonnet slant his nose;
her bag, his baggage; in repose;
with heart both grave and gay.

Over the dunes and far away,
    'twixt Cairo and Deccan;
beneath a palm, beside the Nile,
keeping his crocodilian style
and half an eye on man.

Septuagintennium

For Sir John Betjeman on his 70th birthday

2000 ago of your 70 today
my pen might have pushed at my page
for fame's sake concocting a numerous bouquet
To the laureate voice of his age.

Now — for £5 a line ("At maximum eight,")
true poet of beauties undone,
forgive me for saying no more than, "You're great!"
as I pick up the money and run.

A Prayer to Accompany John Berryman on his Way

The day is gone; the sun does not reach through;
Gray hazes, bloomed with silver, drift among the trees.
No livestock pare, or wheel shall modify,
Or human bombast crackles, hereabout;
But in the slack and fragrant atmosphere,
Murmurs of newly risen water wreathe.
Who stood that vacant temple on the lawn
That disappears beneath the cypresses?
Tall stems, whose white, bud crumpled leaves
Forgetful resin keep, lean on its masonry;
And still as snow slopes in midwinter dusk
Its curtaining.
Centred upon the flags,
(Into whose sleek the eye may dimly reach),
Scattered with winking cushions, featherstitched
Around it bubbed circumference with pix
Establishing the occupant's nativity,
A mammoth ottoman; whose cave retains
A child of three; a fine, plump fingered boy.
You kneel; and in your mind you whisper: Please,
Sweet Sleep, in whom all things find nourishment,
Most kindly principal who bids us leave
Our worries in our clothes, be good to me.

The Poet Mandel'shtam's Debut

Riding the Warsaw/Petersburg express
in late '08, both dressed in upper black,
a woman with her 18-year-old son.

When he was crowned:
"He will be bound to Legal force," she said.
And has since then – not only to herself.
He has in mind
a bondage of a different kind:
to vacant force. For her,
a double worst.

The luggage rack.

"My child, he is the best. His magazine
is seen in Warsaw. What is seen
in Warsaw will, in time, be seen elsewhere.
If he says, yes – then I say yes."

They leave the Petersburg express.

Behold the critic in his chair!
His cuffs are frayed! His mind is bare!

"Madame?" he said. "Good Sir," said she,
"this is my only son and he
thinks what he writes is poetry.
Keenly peruse this sheaf of tommy rot
and tell me: True? Or Not."

"I read them through," the critic wrote,
"I thought them, well... They did not float,

nor did they glide on tender feet.
No head in them, I thought. No beat. No blood:

'An E! An E! And nothing but an E!'

ridiculous, or else
destruction to the breath of God. My God,

I said (but only to myself). Then to herself—
with him the famous barrister inset—
almost began a courteous goodnight,
when by mistake his eyes met mine.

Embarrassment as heavy as Tibet.

To hell with Law, to heaven with Poetry,
I said (but only to myself). And said pro tem:
Madame, your son can write."

"Indeed," said she. Then paused. And then:
"Then when you publish them
he just enough to send his cheque to me."

Urbanal

The slippery whinnock, clear across the way,
has had my tree cut down.
He rang a man who rang a man who knew
a big-boned, broad-backed chap; the type of clay
that stood in red in line at Waterloo.
It took eight hours to knock King Boney down,
and more than 30 years to rear my tree;
but only fifteen dental seconds flat
for that, fat, jelly-baby-faced,
pornocrat to have it stapped.
    Now I can see his house;
a snot-brown, lie-priced, isometric blob,
smack in the middle of my laureate eye.
A yawning house, a stealthily maintained,
and as (God stop his heart) he skives abroad,
a semi-empty house; his swap; who had my tree's
shoulders that made the evening summer breeze
hiss like a milky night-tide up the sand
cut down to save his garage.
    Its roots were getting at his garage.
His garage was endangered. Furthermore,
come autumn, when the bronzed wing in, his car
might get its chrome trim splashed with flock.
    What can I do?
twice 20 000 square in legal blue
behind the leaves that bear his signature
and all my leaves away.

    True, there are quits.
Through the enormous windows of his house
soon after dusk when all was still and glad,
five weeks ago I tingled as I watched
a no less sturdy, somewhat different lad,

slither the cutlery into his bag
and fade; and Sunday last
(meantime his nanny milked my breakfast tea)
his "Me! Me!" squeakers did their peevish best
to baste each other's shop-washed goldilux
with Hong toy Kong posh hand-assembled trucks.
    Such treats, however, will not quash his crime:
indubitably I would have
him and his pimply mouthpiece taken out
put up against that garage wall, and shot —
if all those lads in red and blue were mine.

    And yet I did not know my tree too well.
I did not know its name; its proper age;
whether its leaflike slips of polished silk
were toothed or bayed; or if its full, fresh snood,
brotherly hugged, flushed leek down green imperial;
or did that gust strike dark down adder green? —
how much it gained each year; how high it stood;
or standing might have fetched that fleshy hood,
except he had it lamed, laid, lopped, and logged,
"just for the wood".

    Is there no law?
Can nobody make Somebody obey?
I love the law. I dream about the law.
Few inky maids can make me jaunt so. See:
    An army overspreads a treeless plain.
    A king is up for swaps. Between the lines
    of yet to be committed soldiery,
    leading his horse, alone, a youngish man
    (one of the Lord Protector's *Fervent Best*)
    confronts the Kirkish generals. Flintlocks hiss.
    They bunch. They talk. They separate. They say:
    "Where is your warrant for His Majesty?"
    and hear him, as he draws his sword, say: "This."
    and shamefaced watch him lead brave Charles away.

    Rate me with those who pray
beside the two-years-later headless king;

or cine-see the Emperor rowed away;
some worldoramic, pandimensional fling
stayed by the rape that lies in melody,
and have your own sweet way; but say,
    Go visit City Hall, anonymously
and well prepared; go shaved; go calm; go hat
in humble hand; and,
hot for the dream that scragged regality,
reactivate a hidden bureaucrat,
and with his fuhrerstat
enforce the preservation of your tree;
or will, or may, or might, or soon, or must,
is all you get from me.

    Or say I did; and say,
exploding with authority, I led
a cloud of geriatric minutemen,
lewd, loonie nudists, snagged by plastic leaves,
little old ladies looped to tree-trained dogs,
dogs local, ex-police dogs, Dogs Resist,
a teacher of the Vegetative Tongue
linked to a glamorous preservationist,
two dozen twangling squatters, Puss & Purr,
Bucket disguised, and Dogberry serene,
Blake of The Globe (with its photographer)
plus anyone who likes the colour green,
up to his mammoth sty? Why... fine prepaid,
with well greased sliders wide, that schnorkel he
can tip his fag, look down, and obelise
all my sad riff-raff with impunity.

    A curse upon the law. Where did I kiss
my right to cut that scumbag down goodbye?
If I am weak, and certainly
my eye at sunset can no longer fix
a late bee backing from a mile-off rose,
sly murder haunts my mind; and yet to lie,
for all the world's great-headed blossomers,
one of a long-forgotten laughing stock
locked in a laughing house for aye?

Not bloody me.

Twilight. The blind man's holiday.
Blurred moonshine in the dewy slate.
I am reduced to prayer. I pray:
Let the stump get him. Let him,
you hideous nude, mauve lidded, high-rise sylphs,
whilst he is gruntly drunkling for his key
be lashed by instant withies to the sour
£500000 an acre crud,
stripped of his fancy tat, and left to rot.

Then, when the moon is cooked, and up the way
my neighbour and my neighbour's son perform
Jerusalem (for the umpteenth time) on flute
and English horn,
all through the winking night,
until dear Lucifer is born
again between the courthouse and the block,
and something less than dawn
but more than darkness strides from Ragstone Brock
down and across my city's viewless lea,
crank on his stump I rock,
groaning upon my loss, and on the loss
to local poetry.